BORN ON THE FOURTH OF
JANUARY

A PERSONAL JOURNEY

ERIC BAKER

© ERIC BAKER 2024

You may not, except with our express written permission, distribute or commercially exploit the content. Nor may you transmit it or store it in any other website or other form of electronic retrieval system.

FOREWORD

If it hadn't been for reading my Uncle Stan's memories (U's and Co) which were of him being evacuated during WW2 in the nineteen forties, it never would have occurred to me to have a go at writing something along the same lines. After all, my Gran was born in 1880 and had lived through the most extraordinary times; from horse and cart to walking on the Moon.

My Uncle lived through being evacuated from Bow in East London to a small village in Norfolk, when he was a teenage boy, along with the massive disruption caused by the Second World War. So you will understand that I regarded my lifetime as being of far less interest than theirs. However, after many years of reflection, I decided that the post war years were as turbulent and life changing as the times that had gone before. Added to the fact that him having died, I felt that there would be interest in continuing from where he left off.

I have to say that my style is very different. Whereas my Uncle wrote about actual events and the people involved, I will be telling my story through how national and global events affected the people living at the time. But not as an abstract exercise, I will relate how these national and global events directly led to my personal experiences. What I most definitely do have in common with my Uncle, is that we both lived at a time when our traditional British culture slowly but surely gave way, to the global culture we have today, which is spearheaded by the United States of America.

In appreciation of Uncle Stan's memoirs Us's & Co, along with happy memories of family and friends.

Dedicated To Saint Jude

This book is not a product of academic research, it is written with the authority of someone who lived through the times and was affected by the changes that were taking place.

As such it may not always be historically exact but every effort has been made to avoid factual inaccuracies and it is truthful in essence. After all, facts are not the truth - truth is more than just plain facts.

To borrow from the words of Jane Austin, "This is a post-war history written by a partial, prejudiced and ignorant historian." Eric Baker.

CONTENTS

PREFACE 7

PART ONE
Home From Hospital 9
Crime 15

PART TWO
The Queen's Coronation 17
The Hard Sell 20

PART THREE
National Service 23
The Boy's Brigade 40

PART FOUR
The Big Move 45
Back To School 54

PART FIVE
The Cuban Missile Crisis 58
The Woodstock Festival 65

PART SIX
The Growth of Technology 69
The Walk Home 78

PART SEVEN
Art 82
The Outcomes 91

PART EIGHT
Looking Over My Shoulder 94
Doing My Thing 97

AFTERWORD 99

PREFACE

It is unfortunate that things, without any evidence, often pass into history as facts and becomes the believed normality. So is the case of the nineteen fifties which are often described as a period of gloom and boredom. Black and white films, black and white television, these are the beliefs of those who see all things in black and white. The joy of beating fascism, the growth of technology, the flowering of the arts, the changes in society brought together by fighting together against a common enemy, caused a swelling of optimism and hope. These factors were the beginnings of the most exciting things that we benefit from today. These things are sometimes forgotten.

I was born on the fifth (sic) of January 1949, in the City of London Maternity Hospital, Liverpool Road, Islington. This area of Islington is known as 'The Angel' and this makes me a true 'Cockney' a Cockney is someone born within the sound of the bells of St Mary-Le-Bow. This church, in Cheapside, inside the old City of London walls, is only around a mile away from the Angel, so easily within the sound of the bow bells. There are no longer any maternity hospitals in central London, so us proper Cockneys are few and far between, yet more and more claim to be Cockneys. So beware of imitations.

PART ONE

HOME FROM HOSPITAL

I was taken home to Walford Road in Stoke Newington, where I was to spend my first seven years while growing old enough to become aware of my surroundings. I shared a bedroom with two of my three brothers along with my sister, who had a cot at the side of the room. It was on the second floor and had two wooden sash windows, both looking out onto Walford Road. On the same landing, was our kitchen with its open fire and a large kitchen table.

On the landing going down to the first floor, there was a Butler sink which served as bath for me when I was a toddler. Beneath our bedroom was the living room, a large room with a high ceiling and decorated with a large plaster ceiling rose from which hung an electric light and lampshade.

Our Mum and Dad slept there at night, in a Put-u-Up folding bed which converted to a settee during the day. The room next to living room, was my dad's mum's bedroom, and between her bedroom and her kitchen on the mezzanine level, was our indoor toilet. This part of the house we regarded as belonging to our family.

On the ground floor lived our neighbours (an ageing couple and not part of our family) who had their own three rooms (including another toilet) along with use of the back garden. There was a passage which led to the front door and the small front garden with its privet hedge. Beneath the ground floor was the cellar, a dark and scary space, which extended underneath the pavement, where the coal-hole gave access for delivering the coal. Every room had a fireplace and a no-longer-used gas mantle, although our house was old-fashioned, to my young eyes, everything was perfect. I loved living there.

Our family came to be there because our dad's mum, known as Little Gran, having had been bombed out of her home in the Isle of Dogs, was re-housed there. Our mum and dad joined her later on during the war. Because of the housing shortage, caused by the bombing, local councils often bought up private property and then multi-let them to those in need. So our house was owned by Stoke Newington Borough Council.

Our Relatives

While Little Gran shared our house with us, my mum's family lived less than a mile away in Sandringham Road, Dalston. It was on the other side of the high street and I remember walking there with my two brothers to visit them on a Sunday. Their house, built in the nineteenth century, was once very well to-do but was now owned by Hackney Borough Council. It was a much grander house than ours, with steps leading up to the ground floor, and two further floors above.

Below the ground floor there was, what would have once been, servants' quarters. My mum's mum we called Big Gran, to distinguish her from Little Gran, lived with her youngest son our Uncle Stan (see Us's & Co) and he wasn't married at the time. On the floor below was another uncle with his wife and their two children and on the ground floor was yet another uncle with his wife and their two children. Of course, these young children were our cousins.

It was a custom in those day to give young relatives money and one penny (1d) was the common amount, but Uncle Stan being still unmarred (so wealthy!) would give us a *tanner* (6d) and then ask if that was enough. Enough! It was extremely generous and I'd be straight round to the sweet shop to get it spent. One of my mum's other brothers, Uncle Fred, was killed in Italy where he stood on a land mine. I was told that he was an extremely loved character and was sorely missed by those who knew him. My Big Gran died when I was around four years old but I can still remember her. There were other relatives and at Christmas time, they would come and visit us but I had little idea of who they were. I always assumed they were my dad's relatives, there was a cousin and his wife with their young son, an uncle, a tall angular man who I later learned was a highly respected investigative journalist working for an

Essex newspaper. There were others I had even less idea about, an aunt and some distant cousins from Essex.

Get Togethers

At that time in was common to have a 'party trick' which is something you were good at and was amusing. There was Bertie who performed an Egyptian sand-dance which was absolutely hilarious, an uncle who did magic tricks, Uncle Stan who was a brilliant storyteller, my mum and dad had a mind reading act and little me; I 'died' dramatically in the style of a wild west cowboy who'd just been shot in the stomach. I was already being shaped by what I was seeing on American television imports. Of course, my relatives all loved a sing-song and enjoyed music hall favourites along with popular songs of the thirties and forties. The main criticism I heard of the pop music of the sixties, was that you couldn't hear the words and that you couldn't sing along to them, a situation later remedied with the arrival of karaoke.

Family At Work

Shoreditch has long been the traditional home of furniture makers and as the industry grew, the manufacturers became household names, building factories alongside the River Lea in east London. Our dad grew up in the Isle of Dogs in Poplar and our mum grew up near Roman Road Street Market in the borough of Bow. They met in the nineteen thirties, while both working as French polishers in a furniture factory, got married and moved to Dagenham on the outskirts of London. As well as our mum and dad, all our uncles were employed in the industry either as carpenters or upholsterers.

For a time, Dad worked for a company that made radiograms. A radiogram was a large piece of wooden furniture that included a radio along with a record player. In the event of a fault being reported by a customer, the company would send out a radio engineer to investigate and my dad would go with him in order to 'touch-up' the French polish. Because of this my dad, who had been interested in 'wireless' since being a boy, learnt enough from the engineer to qualify him as an electrician, wiring Wellington bombers during the Second World War.

My earliest memory was of him␣was working for the GPO (General Post Office) as an electrical fitter, a career I was to enter myself. My mum, as was the custom of the day, stayed at home to look after us kids while my eldest brother was away from home doing National Service.

My Big Gran was retired but she had worked as a vegetable cook in the Savoy Hotel.

Notice that I write 'cook' and not 'chef' because in those days the chef (always a man) was in charge of the cooking but did not cook himself. Little Gran was still working as an industrial sewing machinist, making waterproof riding garment for the rich and famous and she carried on at work until she was seventy years of age.

O POINT OF INTEREST

> Uncle Stan started as an upholster but went on to become a salesman and was known to his children as "Stan, Stan the tally man!" From him we got the expression DS. DS meant 'don't serve' and was written, in a discreet place, by salesmen outside certain addresses. DS was to warn fellow salesmen that the occupants of the address were bad payers. So DS became our family term for any disreputable person. He's a right DS!

Our Manor

Walford Road consists of terraced houses, built in a vaguely Georgian style, and runs between Stoke Newington Road in the east and Neville Road in the west. There were just two small blocks of flats built in the spaces left by houses bombed during the war. At the junction of Walford Road and Stoke Newington Road, there was the Walford Arms on one corner and Devonshire Square Baptist Church on the other. At the other end, there was the Walford Road Synagogue on one corner and on the other corner, a small shop which was vacant. Opposite, in Neville Road, there was the Neville Arms and each weekday, at eleven 'o clock, the pub landlord could be found standing in the road, swinging a large hand bell and yelling,

> "Come and get it! Come and get it!"

The coming changes were becoming ever more apparent, at first, us children had the run of the road and could play safely. There was only a handful of cars parked in the road overnight and during the day we only had to make way for a couple of cars each hour. Gradually the teenage boys acquired shiny new bicycles but they didn't go anywhere, they simply rode in circles and performed wheelies for the benefit of admiring onlookers.

There were some old people who sat in their windows watching the world go by, from behind lace curtains. One old woman in particular, made the mistake of coming out one day and telling us off. From then on she was branded a 'witch' and was regularly taunted. Most adults were remarkedly tolerant. One example is when a cricket ball was put through the window of a water board office. When an operative found it, a few days later, he simply handed it back and not a word was said in remonstration. As children, were given a great deal of freedom and you were rarely asked where you had been or what you had been doing. The only rule was that you had to be back home for your mealtime.

Traffic

As the number of cars gradually increased the cobbled streets, very slippery when wet, were covered in tarmac leaving the cobbles in the gutters. I loved it when rainwater gushed through the cobbles and I was ever fascinated by the constant twists and turns. In the winter evenings, the mercury-vapour streetlights cast a soft blue glow that filled my imagination with the mystery of the world around me.

Later as car ownership grew and grew, the new sodium streetlights destroyed the mystery with their harsh yellow light and the streets were no longer the playground of us kids.

Motorbikes

Around this time my dad acquired a motorbike and sidecar (an outfit) which he proudly proclaimed to be 'pre-war' it was usual for many things in those days to be either 'pre-war' or 'post war'. As time went on the same boys, who rode their bicycles aimlessly, on reaching the age of sixteen, acquired motorbikes. There was no need to take a test, with just a provisional licence you could buy a 650cc monster of a machine. Famous names such as AJS, BSA, Norton and Triumph were soon to be seen everywhere. The 'ton-up' (100mph) boys became notorious, racing from Ted's Café on the Southend Road to the roundabout and then back to the café, in the time it took to play a record on the juke box. They gathered at the ACE Café on the North Circular Road, tearing up the tarmac in a similar way. There was the more reckless, doing 'chicken runs' across red traffic lights, causing mayhem. Because of the carnage happening to motor cyclists, the engine size they were allowed, was reduced to 250cc before the test had been passed. Later crash helmets (skid lids) became compulsory but it was to be many years before motorcyclist's lost their notoriety.

Teenagers

At the same time another group of teenage boys were causing trouble, the Teddy Boys. Their hair was styled in an outlandish quiff brought to a shape, at the back of the head, known as a DA (ducks arse) because of its resemblance to a duck's behind! it was also known as a 'Tony Curtis' him being the American film star who made the style popular.

They wore drape jackets, drainpipe trousers and chunky crepe sole shoes known as brothel creepers. They were said to get their inspiration from the dandies of the King Edward VII era. They were famous for gang fights and generally causing trouble. But when you knew them they were just lads having a good, if violent, time and innocent by-standers were perfectly safe. For much of this time I wore a 'Sloppy Joe' Tee-Shirt, together with my hair styled into a 'Crew Cut'. I was treated to a haircut called a 'College Boy' for my fourteenth birthday. All USA inspired.

> **O POINT OF VIEW**
> As I grew older, I often wondered if the teenage madness of those days was due to them growing up during the war.

Crime

It is a truism that most front doors were left unlocked in those days. In our case there was a key on a string that could be reached through the letter box and everyone knew that it was there. But as reports of thefts began to rise, people were beginning to become concerned.

I remember my Uncle saying, "You could leave your front door open pre-war, because you had nothing worth stealing!"

Here was recognition that people had more and more possessions. Keeping hold of them was one of the problems facing an increasingly affluent society.

PART TWO

THE QUEEN'S CORONATION

The earliest memory, that I can put a date on, is the Queen's coronation in 1953 and the street party that celebrated it. It's well known that the coronation caused a sharp rise in the popularity of television and I had noticed that suddenly there were rooftop television aerials everywhere. However my dad had a life-long interest in radio and television and so he had bought a television in 1948, a year before I was born, so I would have been among the first not knowing what life was like before television. Made by Pye, it had a nine-inch screen, displayed only in black and white and the only programmes it could receive were broadcast by the BBC. It cost £60 which was around eight week's wages and equates to around £4,800 today.

So I do remember friends and relatives gathered around the tiny screen and I remember most of all, the street party and afterwards playing in our back garden with our downstairs neighbour's granddaughter. I'd never seen her before and I've never seen her since. The idea that everyone knew everyone is a misconception, at least it was where we lived.

Day to Day Life

Although coronation day stands out, most of my memories are of a much more prosaic (but no less interesting) nature. The working day consisted of my dad going off in the morning to work his forty-five hours week, my two brothers going to school and my mum being at home to look after my sister and me. It amazes me that many people think that life is harder now than it's ever been previously.

Washing day meant just that – a day! Not the moments it takes to fill a washing machine. There was the giant bar of carbolic soap, the washboard and mangle for removing the excess water before hanging the clothes on the washing line. That washing line was the start of my interest in all things mechanical. It fascinated me that with the aid of pulley arrangement, fixed outside the second storey window, along with a second pulley, fixed to a pole in the garden, the washing could be attached to the line using clothes pegs. The line could be pulled along, to hang out or bring in the clothes, without putting a foot in the garden. Well, *I* found interesting anyway!

My mum must have noticed my interest in mechanical things, because she bought me a toy watch. In those days, toys were unbelievably unsophisticated compared to today but even so, I was totally unimpressed. The hour hand and the minute hand were permanently fixed to each other in a relationship of ninety degrees, making it impossible to accurately represent the time. I complained to my mum and told her that there was a much better version where, although still a toy, the hands could be moved realistically just like in a real watch. She agreed to buy me one when had I learned to stop using the potty and learned to use the lavatory. Clever old mum, introducing me to multi-tasking at a very young age, and so my very next task was to learn to use the lavatory and then learn how to tell the time! Game on!

Going Shopping

A regular activity was going to the shops in the high street. In those days, there were no supermarkets, no 'fridges and no cars, so the shopping was done Little and often. We had the famous chain stores such as Marks & Spencer, Woolworths, Home & Colonial and the Cooperative Wholesale Society (CWS, now Coop). In the CWS, as a customer, you were a shareholder and entitled to share of the profits. These profits were known as the 'dividend' and so in any transaction your dividend number was recorded. Such was the importance attached to this number (in our case, 775493) that my siblings and I have never forgotten it.

The Corner Shops

The majority of shops were privately owned or part of a small family empire and the sales assistants served you from behind a counter. I enjoyed the friendly banter and my mum could give as good as she got, it was all good fun and made shopping a pleasure. The back streets were full of shops as well, there was at least twenty within a ten minute walk from our house.

Although these small shops came to be called convenience stores there wasn't much convenience about them in those days. Closed all day Sunday, half day closing Thursday (where we lived), closed for lunch and closed for the whole day, which was either late in the afternoon or in the early evening. From American films we saw how easy shopping was there, self-service, stacked with food and open all day and every day. Despite the poor quality of the early stores, supermarkets would soon be on their way.

Of course, I acknowledge that supermarkets have improved beyond recognition over the years and have become an indispensable part of the community. However, I still use the small independent retailers as often as possible. They keep me in touch with the memory of shopping with my mum and the old-fashioned Stoke Newington High Street, as it was then.

O POINT OF INTEREST

Long before decimalisation and the inflation of the seventies, there was a completely different concept of the value of money. The basic unit of currency was the pound but everyday items cost far less than this amount, so the shilling was the practical base unit and most prices were expressed in shillings and pence. There were 240 old pence (d) to the pound (£1). To give an idea of how far values have changed, in those days a chocolate Mars Bar costs 4d, so you could buy sixty of them for £1. Today you would just about get *one*!

Street Markets

One of the joys of going to street markets was listening to the market trader's patter. Patter is the trader's line of chat, which combined with highly dexterous handling of the goods, almost like juggling, is intended to persuade you to buy. However, the arrival of supermarkets brought with it an increase in consumer protection and, although generally to be welcomed, this was a shame because it brought to an end the market trader's entertaining but outrageous patter.

Brick Lane

In my experience Brick Lane was the best market in London to visit on a Sunday morning. I'd go there to watch, listen, learn and maybe pick myself up a bargain! There were some very talented stall holders, always interesting, always cheeky, always hugely entertaining and often downright hilarious. The crowd would join in the banter, everyone giving as good as they got, all far more natural than a tedious comedian's observational rants and the knowing, sycophantic laughter of their audiences.

The Hard Sell

A common technique was to invent a fantastic but plausible story, describing how the stall holder had been forced to sell his stock at crazy, give-away prices. Then the first items would be sold at ridiculously low prices, starting a feeding frenzy, with the first customers almost begging to spend their money. What the unaware wouldn't know, was that these first purchasers were 'stooges' who worked for the stall holder. Having been to the market several times, I had the experience to keep my eyes open and watch the first lucky buyers, jubilantly walking away with their 'snips' (ridiculously cheap bargains) only to return unobtrusively, a little while later, and surreptitiously return their 'purchases' to the stallholder's stock.

Of course, these traders had to make a living and that meant making bona-fide sales. So, after the first rush was over, genuine purchasers were sold the goods at realistic prices, probably cheaper than the shops, and everyone was happy.

O POINT OF VIEW

> Over the years, I came to understand that nobody was fooling anybody. The customers knew that they hadn't got a snip, they'd paid a fair price and got value for money. Otherwise they wouldn't go back. The market traders knew that nobody believed their patter but it served as a form of advertising, bringing crowds of people to their stall, knowing that some of them would make a purchase. The point is that everyone had a good time and everyone understood the deal. Madison Avenue — you ain't got nuthin' on old Brick Lane!

PART
THREE

NATIONAL SERVICE

I stated before that I shared my bedroom with two of my brothers, the third brother was away from home doing National Service. The first time I saw my eldest brother was when a handsome young man in a soldier's uniform came through the door and gave me a huge grin.

"Say hello to your brother, Eric!" Mum beckoned.

My brother and I grinned at each other and probably said hello, but I don't remember. So this is what's in store for me, I must join the army one day. My brother was born in 1936 and so it would have been 1954 when he became eighteen and eligible for national service. In later years he would tell me how he had a great time, spent mostly riding a motorcycle and running messages with him being in the Royal Signals Corp.

All Present and Correct

Of course at that time a whole generation was doing National Service known as the 'cake' (I don't know why) and the greatest legacy, it seemed to me, was that they learned how to iron a shirt. Over subsequent years, I have many times observed these veterans gathered at the pub, ageing disgracefully, overweight in their elasticated trousers, generally crumpled but as proud as punch in their immaculately ironed shirts. Smoother than a billiard ball with creases sharper than a Gurkha's kukri, in their minds they are on parade standing smartly to attention. They should all be given a medal; an *Iron* Cross perhaps? No, perhaps not.

Home on Leave

However, not everyone enjoyed national service and we had a neighbour who regularly failed to return from leave, going awol as it's known. For onlookers the fun would start when the miliary police stopped outside his address and knocked on the front door. I remember once watching from an upstairs window and seeing the MPs arrive at the front door and seeing our reluctant hero desperately scrambling over the garden walls at the back. The MPs simply waited at each end of our road and nabbed him when he was forced to exit on reaching the last garden. These escapades were a source of great fun for us and, I reckon, secretly enjoyed by the MPs.

Draft Dodging

When it came to my next eldest brother's turn, he failed the army medical and so would not be accepted for national service. Naturally my mum was concerned and together they went to see our GP. The GP told her it was just a technicality and nothing to worry about. When my mum insisted on knowing the details, the GP retorted sharply,

"What, do you want him to go in the army?"

My mum got the message. National Service was coming to an end and failing conscripts, on medical grounds, was one way of bringing this ending about.

Royal Signals Cap Badge

> ## ○ POINT OF VIEW
>
> The ending of National Service, in 1960, also resolved one of my early dilemmas. Even at my young age, I often considered whether it was better to be born a boy or a girl. If you were a boy you had to join the army but if you were a girl, you had babies. With the ending of national service, I no longer had to join the army but girls still had babies, so that decided it. I was glad to be born a boy - no contest. Sorry girls!

ERIC BAKER

The Local Eateries

As I was growing older, I became more aware of my surroundings and began to take things in. Not far away was our local sweet shop, Pagliaro's which was run by a middle-aged Italian couple as you might guess from the name. As well as a full range of sweets, some sold loose in jars in 4oz portions, others priced to suit our pockets, penny chews, etc. Being Italian they naturally made their own ice cream; vanilla when served with a chocolate flake became a 99, and lemon Ice with traces of lemon peel, when served with a chocolate flake became a 66.

In the next street was our fish and chip chop (never called a 'chippie' that's a northern term) and was notable for its coal-fired range that looked as if it was falling apart, a suspicion borne out by finding a large rivet among the chips one day. A small portion of chips was 4d and a large portion 6d. There was a choice of fish which included: rock eel, rock salmon, cod, plaice, wing skate and middle skate. In those days, it was wise not to buy fish and chips before Monday's lunch time as you would be given Saturday's re-heated leftovers!

> ○ **POINT OF INTEREST**
>
> A common misconception is that fish and chips was wrapped in newspapers. This is not really true. The first layer around the food was grease proof paper, the next layer was white paper and then finally newspaper. But not *used* newspaper, these were newspapers that had remained unsold and so a secondary use was found for them. This is now known as re-using.

Pie and mash was also very popular and we had an excellent shop in Dalston. The pies are very special and nothing like the ones sold elsewhere. There were live eels slithering in a bath of shallow water from which was made jellied eels (a delicacy if you like eating fish bones) and combining the eel juice with parsley made the 'liquor' poured over your pie and mash. Proper pie and mash can only be found in London and makes a cheap and delicious meal, to this day. There was also pease (yellow split peas) pudding and saveloys sold loose, so you took your own pudding bowl, and they would fill it with whatever you bought.

Working Men's Cafes

Although eating out was not the norm, there was enough demand to justify a small provision of working men's cafes. These were named from the road, the area or the name of the owner. Our local one was The Apollo, otherwise known as 'handlebars' on account of the proprietor's moustache.

There you could get meals throughout the day, starting with breakfast, midday meals and then tea and cakes in the late afternoon. The unstated rules were that you ordered a meal at mealtimes and that you did not linger if they were busy. Apart from the consideration, that the owners needed to make a living, you could come and go as you please. Being typical Italians, the owners provided a cheerful and efficient service and was the first, that I am aware of, to purchase an Espresso coffee machine. This gleaming piece of hissing, chromium provided glamour and attracting the local 'hounds' (teddy boys and girls) and initiated the movement from the English habit of drinking tea to the American, and Italian, habit of drinking coffee. Espresso coffee, mixed with hot milk, became known as 'froffy coffee' by the foreign-language-loving customers.

> ## O POINT OF INTEREST
> A typical breakfast consisted of egg and bacon (not bacon and eggs), tomatoes, baked beans and fried slice (of bread). A midday meal could be roast beef and two veg (which included boiled potatoes and gravy), pork chop and chips or omelette and chips. All this was homemade and cooked on the premises with not a beefburger in sight. Wimpey's was the first to lead the charge of the beef burger onslaught.

Charlies Cafe

> ○ **POINT OF VIEW**
>
> If you wanted a quick snack, you would have a thick slice of buttered toast. That is *butter* and not the by-product of making axle grease, known as margarine. Despite the advertising claims, I *can* tell the difference. Really easily!

Along with traditional food, scattered thinly along the high street, were Chinese, French and Italian restaurants serving anglicised versions of their cuisine for those who thought themselves sophisticated. These establishment often advertised themselves in the local cinemas and the dream-like, other-worldly, quality of the adverts and the jaunty commentary, made them very memorable. They always finished with the enticement that they were only a short walk from the cinema.

Avoiding School

It was during this time that I began to realise that I would soon be starting primary school. I tried reasoning with my mum, explaining that there was no need for me to go to school. After all, I was learning lots of things at home; I could use the lavatory, I could tell the time, I could tie my own shoelaces and although I only looked at the pictures in comics, I pretended that I could read. Then one day, something happened that forced me to *actually* learn to read.

Learning to Read

One day, in the Beano, the character Rodger the Dodger (an early source of inspiration for me) was reading a comic as part of the story. Now there is nothing so calculated to spark a child's interest, than seeing a character behaving in the same way as a child. The problem was that although I could see that this tiny, comic within a comic had proper lettering, I was unable to understand the words. So I asked my brother what the letters said,

> *"They're not proper letters they don't say anything, you can't print things that small."*

But I could see that they were proper letters and so the only way to prove it, would be to learn to read them. In our bedroom was a sweet tin that had large very clear letters on it. One day on waking up, I saw these letters and asked my brother what they said,

"Hacks for Throat and Chest." He told me.

Duly noted I let this digest and on the next day I asked again,

"Hacks for Throat and Chest." He told me again.

On the third day I asked yet again,

"Okay for the last time, Hacks for Throat and Chest!"

I didn't feel that I could ask him again and so on the fourth day, when I woke up, I looked at the letters with determination. Then the magic happened.

Hacks for Throat and Chest, I read. *Yes, read!* Suddenly the words suddenly became something I could understand. I can't explain the shift between *seeing* words and *reading* words but many people have told me of having a similar experience. So from now on, there was no stopping me and with the help of Rupert the Bear, whose stories are told in three ways, like the Rosetta Stone, a whole world of books had opened up to me.

My Mum is Not Convinced

Despite my now really being able to read my reasoning, reinforced with some industrial-strength wheedling, still failed to convince my mum that I didn't need to go to school. Although very kindly, she could also be very determined when needed and so one day she tried a little subterfuge,

"Come on Eric, we're going to Dalston to do some shopping." This meant walking by the primary school and as we approached the playground she said,

"Look there's your brother, let's called him over."

My brother duly came running over with a suspiciously big grin on his face. Even at my young age I suspected that this meeting didn't happen by chance. We stayed and chatted for a while, I can't remember exactly what was said, but it would have been along the lines of how wonderful school is, so much fun and how I'd love it! I was very glad to see my brother and after our brief chat, my Mum and I needed to carry on shopping,

"Well, did you enjoy seeing your brother?" My mum asked as we walked away.

"Yes, but I still don't want to go to school."

We were walking side by side, so I didn't see the expression on my mum's face. But I could guess.

Starting Infant School

The rule was you had to go to school when you are five years old. This was generally interpreted as starting school in the *September of the school year that you become five*. My persistence in not wanting to go to school must have partially worked, because my mum decided that I would not start school until the *term* in which I became five so I started infants school in January 1954.

To this day, I do not know why she relented and I'm not sure that it was a good idea. The problem was that the other pupils had known each other since September and had formed friendships, whereas I stood out like a sore thumb because of not knowing anyone.

The First Day

Anyway on that first day, I was taken into the classroom and given a place to sit and given a book to read. As I remember, the other children were all reading and, although I can't remember in detail, the time passed by pleasantly enough. I'd assumed the book was mine to keep and so it was a bit of a shock when at the end of the morning, the book monitor came round and collected all the books.

Mum was waiting outside the playground to take me home for lunch (we called it dinner) and as we walked along she asked me,

"Well, did you enjoy going to school?"
"It was alright, it was not as bad as I thought."

I'm sure she felt that was as good as it's going to get from me.

After I had eaten, it was time to go back to school and although I didn't want to go back, I didn't make the performance I'd made when first going in the morning.

In those days you could leave school at fifteen but I remember my parents saying that they wanted all of us to stay on until sixteen and get some school qualifications.

I must have accepted that I'd stay on for the extra year because when my gran greeted me, at the end of the first day, and asked me,

> "Hello Rick (her nickname for me) did you like going to school today?"

"It was alright," I replied reluctantly before adding dolefully, "oh well, only eleven more years to go."

A Typical Day at School

Walking from home to school, with my mum, took about fifteen minutes. The journey involved walking to the high street, turning right, crossing four side streets, before arriving at the derelict Alexandra Theatre, that stood on the corner of Princess May Road, and then crossing over to the gates of Princess May Primary School. Although there was much less traffic then, the roads were far more dangerous than they are today and road safety was instilled into children from the earliest age. I still remember the kerb drill for crossing the road; look right, look left, look right again and if the road is clear, cross the road.

Princess May School, a Victorian building, consisted of mixed infants on the ground floor, junior girls on the first floor and junior boys on the second floor. To the front and to the rear of the main building, were the playgrounds enclosed by a mixture of brick walls and fencing. The school and its surroundings extended a quarter of the way back from the high street, between Princess May Road and Barretts Grove.

School Dinners

At the back of the rear playground, on most days the reek of boiled cabbage drifted from the single storey building which housed the dining hall. In order to get your dinner you had to join the queue and as you walked along the counter, holding your dinner tray, your meal would be dolloped onto your plate by one of the dinner ladies.

Before you sat down another dinner lady, and **one particular** dinner lady, would pour gravy all over your food. This particular dinner lady was an ostentatiously strict disciplinarian, a real Dickensian throw back. Small and shabbily dressed, her ill-fitting hat held in place with a giant skewer of a hat pin. Probably lacking any real schooling herself, she was constantly shouting and haranguing us kids. Her driving motivation was to show herself unimaginably superior to us kids and when you had done something wrong, in her mind at least, that would be her excuse to zap you with the full force of her disdain. In what she believed to be educated English, she would single you out leaving you in no doubt of your insignificance,

"What are you a doing of?" Bellowed in her poshest East-End accent.

To that there could be no reply and none was expected, such was its withering power.

One day, this dinner lady was busy shouting at some poor kid and so not paying attention to the job she was actually paid to do, that is pouring the gravy. My sister had got her meal and, as she passed with the plate the dinner lady, without looking, poured gravy all over my sister's *salad*. That's right salad! When this was pointed out to her, she made no acknowledgement of what she had done and simply waved my sister off to sit down and eat it. I later said to my sister you should have asked her,

"What are you a doing of?"

My sister and I often laugh at this memory of great old school dinners.

Gaining Independence

When I first started school, I was going home for my dinner and Mum would come and fetch me from school and then take me back to school after we had eaten. It didn't take me long to notice that the other kids were coming and going, without their parents, and one day as we crossed the final road to school, I shook my hand from hers,

> "Mum, I'm old enough to go to school on my own it's embarrassing."

She didn't answer and continued to take me to school for several days more. I noticed that sometimes, as we crossed a side road, she would let go of my hand. Then one day she said,

> "I've decided that you can go to school without me but you can't go on your own," I waited to hear what would come next, "I've asked the girl who lives next door, and she said that she'd take you."

Hmm, not exactly what I had in mind but I had no choice other than to accept. So the next day, outside the garden gate, there were two young girls waiting for me and we all set off together. One of the girls I already knew and the other was her friend, they were not much older than me and didn't seem too keen on my tagging along. Any reservations I had quickly became a reality, these two girls just loved to talk and talk to each other. They were so keen on talking that they would often forget to walk! On the times they didn't forget to walk, they would dawdle and for me this snail's pace was intolerable, at least my mum walked briskly. So it was time to start some well-practised wheedling again,

> "Mum, do I have to go to school with those girls? They spend all their time talking and I'm just left hanging about, it's really boring. I'm alright to walk on my own, you've shown me what to do."

Well much to my relief and with a kindly smile, Mum agreed to let me walk to school on my own. Previously while walking with my mum, as we walked to school together, I'd noticed that she sometimes let go of my hand but I never realised that she was testing me. Many years later she told me that the first time I walked to school alone, she had secretly followed me from a distance. It was only when she was satisfied that I did cross the roads safely, that I was given the full go ahead to be let off the reins. Thanks, Mum!

First Steps to Independence

I really appreciated the freedom I'd been given; I could come and go as I pleased with the only rule being home in time for tea. And she was not alone, all of my mates enjoyed the same kind of freedoms and, above all, freedom from over protection! It still surprises me how much freedom we had. We played on bomb sites, in derelict buildings, we often cycled, we got as far as Epping Forest, Potters Bar and even St Albans. We played in the streets and we played in the parks. We went to the Geffrye Museum (where we allowed to paint and draw), to the Science Museum, the Victoria and Albert Museum and the Tower of London, all without adult supervision.

After many years of enjoying all this freedom, I grew curious and one day it came up naturally to ask,

> *"Mum, don't you worry about me when I'm off out somewhere?"*

She thought for a moment,

> *"Of course I worry, but I trust you and I wouldn't be a very good mother if I stopped you from playing with your friends."*

Those words impressed me more than anything that's ever been said to me. That was the kind of selfless love typical of my mum and, it must be said, typical of my friend's mums as well.

Junior School

My time in school passed pleasantly enough, the lessons were interesting and I got on fairly well so there's little to report until the third year of juniors, when we got a new class teacher.

In the 1950s many teachers had been in the armed services and had fought during the war. In our school, the headmaster had been a submarine captain and our class teacher had been a bomber pilot. With his curly black hair and dark moustache, he certainly looked the part and he was what is known as an 'inspirational' teacher but he was certainly not a Mr Chips!

In my third year of junior school there were around sixty pupils. Our classroom was set out in ten rows of twin desks with an aisle in the centre for the teacher to walk up and down. A teaching assistant was unheard of. There was a desk at the front for the teacher and, alongside his desk, a blackboard and easel. We still used the old-style pen and nib, so desks had ink wells and the lids opened for us to store our books. You sat at your desk during the lessons and you could do very little, except staying put, without putting your hand up and given permission by the teacher.

This rigid arrangement was a necessary part of discipline because, as any teacher will tell you, there's a lot of them and only one of you, and children in a group can easily become very unruly. Not that our teacher had many problems in this area. He had a three-stage disciplinary procedure. Starting with sarcasm (bless his little cotton socks), next mocking (if I can get here on time from Greenwich and you are late and only live round the corner) and finally anger. His closing the classroom door may not sound much, but it was very isolating and very menacing both threatened and in actuality.

> ### ◯ POINT OF INTEREST
> I only remember one instance of corporal punishment at primary school and this was given for truancy, not for misbehaviour in the classroom. This was administered by the class teacher, with the pupils and head teacher looking on. It involved two strokes of the cane on each hand and the main purpose was to force home the message, not to cause undue pain. The pupil, duly chastened, then rejoined the class. To describe the cane as being physically 'beaten' is a gross exaggeration and a misuse of the English language.

Although our teacher was a strict disciplinarian, he made the lessons interesting and went far above and beyond what was expected in the classroom in those days. We learned French (normally a secondary school subject, we did a 'topic' (mine was about sugar) which allowed us the freedom to leave the classroom and research in the library unsupervised. We formed a class recorder group and staged a performance of Elizabethan Serenade for our parents on open day. The favoured boys at the front of the class (the teacher's pets) could sometimes persuade him to relate anecdotes from his experiences of being a bomber pilot during the war, this enthralled us all and brightened the lesson immeasurably. Being young, we associated his stories with heroism not with death and destruction.

Mixed Juniors

Despite all these positive attributes there were times when he could be very petty. The worst example of this was when, in the final year of juniors, we changed from being a boys' juniors and became a mixed Juniors. This involved half of us boys staying on the second floor, while half of the girls from the first floor came up and joined us. Our teacher divided the class into boys on the left and girls on the right. Because of the way the numbers worked out, I found myself in the centre of the classroom sharing a desk with one of the girls. Unsurprisingly the teacher's pets were well inside the group of boys but it is what the teacher said, that amazes me to this day,

"I don't believe in mixed education; girls should look after the home and there's no place for you in my classroom. I'm not going to teach girls; you must get by the best you can without any help from me."

Even in those days if the head teacher had heard what was said, he would have been in serious trouble but he was as good as his word and totally acted as if the girls weren't there. I later found his disdain would extend to me, along with the girls.

The Eleven Plus Exam

In junior school we weren't normally given homework but as the Eleven Plus approached, the teacher gave us extra work to take home. It wasn't compulsory, but he made it very clear that you couldn't pass the exam without making that extra effort. So I dutifully took the assigned work home with me on the first night. Walking along close to my home, carrying a satchel for the first time, I was afraid that my friends would think me a swot and I became acutely embarrassed. The thought of being embarrassed far outweighed the benefits of passing any exam. This combined with the horrible thought of taking schoolwork into my home and so I gave the homework a miss. I wasn't that keen on going to a grammar school anyway some friends, already at grammar school had warned me about the amount of homework you were given to do. On the next day, when I didn't hand any work in, the teacher gave me a look but he said nothing. I could see from his face, that he now thought of me in the same way as he thought of the girls.

Passing The Eleven Plus Exam

I don't remember much about taking the eleven plus but, having dismissed it from my mind, I was horrified to be told that I had passed. Of course my teacher wasn't impressed, because I had passed despite not having done his homework. From then on, he never wasted an opportunity to ask me a difficult question and when I didn't know the answer, he would delight in his weapon of ridicule,

"There goes the grammar schoolboy, he doesn't know the answer. Ah, bless his little cotton socks!"

Said to raise a laugh from the apple polishers and they would gleefully oblige. Even his final year-end report was dismissive, it was really negative and didn't mention my passing the eleven plus.

Goodbye Mr Chips

Despite this pettiness, I will always remember him as a brilliant teacher. He went far beyond the 'chalk and talk' style of the day and his lessons were unfailingly interesting. He was frightening and challenging in the same measure and all of us pupils admired him. Not just us but also his colleagues and to see all the mums clamouring around him, eager to discuss their children, was an education in itself! As for those girls he ignored, how did they get on? I'm delighted to say that three of them passed the eleven plus which was in line with the national average. So maybe they didn't need him or maybe some of his magic rubbed off on them? I've no way of knowing. The only thing I know for sure is that, despite my not doing the homework he set, I would never have passed the eleven plus but for him being an exceptional teacher.

The Brown Bear, Leman Street

> ○ **POINT OF VIEW**
>
> The passing of the 1944 Education Act dramatically changed education for the better, although it didn't seem like that to us young kids at the time. I was monumentally unfair in my attitude to school because all I wanted to do was to start work. As with many others, of a practical leaning, who wanted to work with their hands and resented being made to sit at a desk.
>
> All because of the snobbish belief that academic achievement is far superior to everything else.
>
> I now realise the many benefits of my education but I am still absolutely resolute in my certain belief, that academic achievement is not the be all and end all. There are many different kinds of ability and we need them all.

Sunday School

At around the same time as starting junior school, I also began to attend Sunday school at our local church. Devonshire Square Baptist Church got its name from Devonshire Square in Stepney, where it was first sited, and it stood on the corner of the Walford Road and the High Street. During the war, the main building of the church was hit by an incendiary bomb and so our meetings were in the adjacent church hall. My mate Kenny and I, both loved mucking about and getting up to mischief. Our biggest adventure was finding a door that gave access to the ruined part of the church, where we would stealthily go exploring.

Of course the adults never found out what we were up to and, apart from the mischief, I liked going to Sunday school because I enjoyed studying the bible stories.

The Scripture Union Exam

Each year the Scripture Union chose a part of the bible to set as an exam topic, which we then studied as a group, guided by the Sunday school teacher. Although we were young, we had many interesting discussions and I learned to listen to different points of view. This helped me to arrive intelligently at my own opinions and not just believe whatever I'm told. When the time came, we would sit an external exam and then have to wait for the results.

Naturally the goal was to pass, but the special challenge was to score one hundred percent. If you achieved this, you had your name sign-written in gold letters on a large wooden panel. One of my classmates achieved it every year and I'm proud to say that I also achieved it, but only the once.

> **O POINT OF INTEREST**
>
> In 1955 the Borough Council offered us the house we lived in for around eighty pounds, which was equivalent to about ten weeks wages. Walford Road is still easily recognisable and houses similar to the one we turned down, are on the market for around £1.7m!

> **O POINT OF INTEREST**
>
> Of all the events that took place in the 1950s, that I've to be thankful for, was the passing of the Clean Air Act in 1954. Prior to that, the poisonous atmosphere, largely caused by the burning of coal in domestic fire-places and electricity power stations, caused the notorious 'pea-souper' smogs that London became famous for. These crippling smogs killed thousands and left many, like me, struggling to breathe. A side benefit of the clean air act was that the many soot-blackened public buildings could be cleaned, leaving them as we see them today.

The Boy's Brigade

I also joined the Boy's Brigade where I learned to play the bugle, very badly, and learned how to march properly. Once a month we had a band parade marching through the streets, it may sound very military but it wasn't really. Although it wasn't to everybody's taste. One Sunday morning, a fellow in a string vest threw banana skins at us from an upstairs window. Serves him right it wasn't early, it was eleven o' clock, he shouldn't have gone to bed so late the previous night.

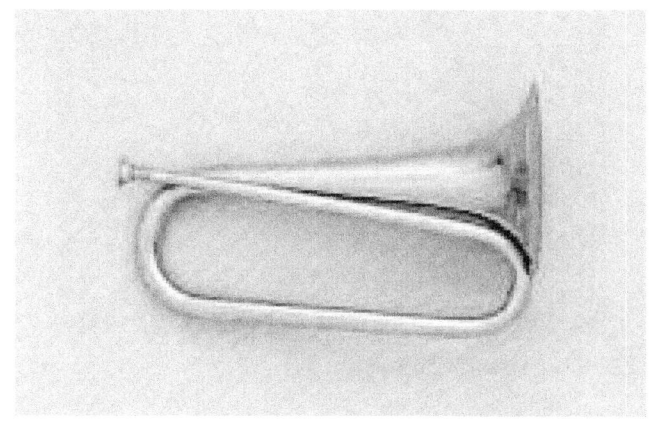

Brass Bugle

My family on holiday by the seaside in 1949 (I'm the baby).

The Queen's coronation street party 1953. Mum (white blouse) and Dad are standing on the left and I'm bottom right.

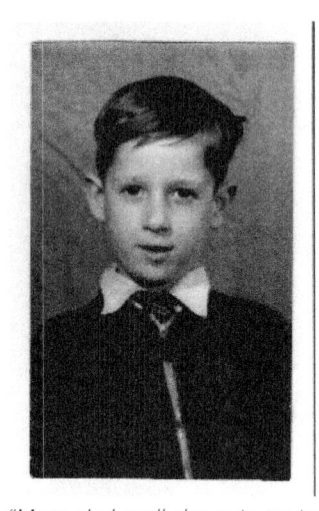

"Mum, do I really have to go to school?"

"I told you that I'd hate school!"

'Pre-war' Panther sidecar outfit.

Future 'ton-up' boy

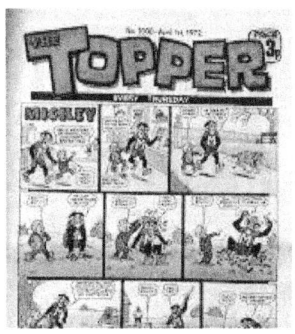

British Comic 1963

American Comic 1963

Ford Zephyr 1963

Ford Mustang 1963

PART
FOUR

THE BIG MOVE

For some time, there had been talk of us moving and it became obvious that something was brewing because my mum, normally calm and unflustered, was becoming very agitated and often repeated,

> "We've been on the housing list for over twenty-two years, at last it looks like something is happening!"

What was happening is that we were being offered a four-bedroom flat, in a small new housing development called Burma Court Estate. The estate was in Clissold Crescent, which is not far from Walford Road. However there was a hiccup, because Mum was insisting that Dad's Mum (Little Gran) must be given a place near to the rest of us. Happily, with the help of the borough council, we were offered another flat, for Little Gran, which was only a short walk away from ours. So, there was only one more thing to be resolved - did us kids want to move? It is to their everlasting credit that our parents, together with all of us, held a 'council of war' in order to discuss the pros and cons of moving or staying where we are. I remember the facts being presented and being held up for discussion. I loved Walford Road and knew nothing else, so I wanted to stay put but, realising my lack of knowledge, I kept my gob shut and resigned myself to going with the flow.

Looking back, many years later, I wondered what on earth were my Mum and Dad doing, what was there to talk about? Staying in three rooms in a decaying building, sleeping in a Put-u-Up, having house mice (a vicious, destructive version of field mice!) and climbing up and down stairs all day.

Alternatively, move to nice modern ground floor flat with four bedrooms, a living room, a purpose-built kitchen, and a bathroom with hot and cold running water. What was there not to like! So together we made a unanimous decision the best thing was to move. Clever old Mum and Dad! Now us kids could not complain later that we were forced to move. So, in nineteen fifty-seven we were on the move from one side of Stoke Newington to the other side. A journey of around ten minutes on foot and the journey of a lifetime for me.

> **O POINT OF INTEREST**
> We were offered the chance to buy our house from the council for £80 around but the offer was declined because of the maintenance costs and the sitting tenants. Houses in the same road are on the market for around £1.4 million today!Burma Court Estate

When Little Gran was bombed out of her house in the Isle of Dogs, she was offered the house in Walford Road. However it came with the caveat, that while not as bad as the London docks, it was still in a bombing area because of being near to Dalston Junction railway station. Sharing the pragmatic attitudes of the times (if it's got your number on it!) she brushed all safety considerations aside and remarked to the effect, what is the point of being safe when you have nowhere to live?

Around Clissold Crescent, as Walford Road, there was much evidence of destruction, either in the form of bomb sites or in the form of newly built council flats.

Our new flat was in one of the seven small blocks, that formed the Burma Court Estate. The estate was built on a human scale, unlike many other estates that brought destruction and havoc to their communities. There were no cars permitted in the estate, we knew our neighbours and we had a kindly caretaker who had the endless task of keeping us 'dustbin lids' in line. Despite this being inner London, there were no geezers, no gangsters and no descendants of royalty, just us fun loving kids who had our hearts in the right place.

> ○ **POINT OF INTEREST**
>
> The estate was named after the Burma Campaign fought during WW2 and the blocks of flats, called houses, were named after places in Burma or the heroes of the campaign. So: Lashio, Mandalay, Rangoon, Karen, Wingate, Chindit and Orde Houses.
>
> NOTE: In 1989, Burma changed its name to Myanmar but the estate retains its original name.

Clissold Crescent

Clissold Crescent is a curved road (as the name suggests) that lies between Stoke Newington High Road to the east and Green Lanes to the west, so between the old boroughs of Hackney and Islington. It was clearly built in a more prosperous past, many of the Victorian houses were built with servants' quarters and the crescent was lined with plane trees. To the north there is Clissold Park and along Stoke Newington Church Street there are Georgian houses once lived in by the rich and famous.

There is the gothic-revival style Victorian parish church (St Marys) with its towering steeple and, on the other side of the road, the original St Marys dating back to eleventh century. A bit further along, is Stoke Newington Town Hall, a splendid example of a nineteen thirties civic building.

New River is an artificial waterway constructed in the time of King James 1. It originates in Hertfordshire, flows through Clissold Park (now underground) then, at the back of Burma Court Estate, it continues on its way to the Angel, Islington. Its purpose was to provide drinking water for the City of London. So, although we lived in a council flat, we were surrounded by history and fine architecture. Stoke Newington, to this day, is one of the most interesting and historic areas of London.

North Versus East

It's one of life's irritations is when people, who have little knowledge of London, spread wrong information. In particular, Stoke Newington *is not in East London*. Its post code is N16 or N4, *the letter 'N' indicating north being the clue*. In 1965, Stoke Newington and Shoreditch were merged together with Hackney, to form the New London Borough of Hackney. So because Stoke Newington comes under the administrative jurisdiction of Hackney, it is now often said to be in East London. However, a change in administration does not mean a change in geography, as a look on a map will quickly and easily indicate. And while we're on the subject nobody who grew up in Stoke Newington, *to my certain knowledge*, has ever called it 'Stokey'.

> ○ **POINT OF INTEREST**
>
> Although not precisely defined, for those who grew up in London, the East End is the historic boroughs of Stepney and Bethnal Green. Having the post codes of E1 and E2, it is bounded by the Tower of London, Bishopsgate, the River Thames, and the borough of Bow. The new London Borough of Tower Hamlets (Stepney, Bethnal Green & Bow) is now accepted as being the East End. That's it - not the whole of East London, not Essex, not Hertfordshire, just Tower Hamlets.

Secondary School

Having passed the eleven plus exam, I now faced a huge problem. Although my parents were never pushy, they naturally felt that I should apply to Hackney Downs Grammar School (formerly Grocers). Friends had warned me about the amount of homework to do, plus it was on the other side of Hackney Downs, so going to that school would entail nearly an hour's walk or a change of two buses. When I am out of my depth, I go 'head down – arse up' and simply plough ahead. So as Mum had arranged an interview with the school, I obediently went along with it.

We arrived and were asked to wait in the foyer before meeting the headmaster. I immediately knew that, despite loving public school stories, this was my worst nightmare coming true. It wasn't just the wood panelling, it wasn't just the masters in their mortar boards and gowns, it was the air of industry and determination that scared the hell out of me.

If I am interested in something, I can apply myself at least as well as anyone else but *if I am not interested*, my motivation vanishes quicker than a news reader's smile when the cameras are turned off. So the interview was doomed before it began. My memory has protected me from what actually happened in the interview, let's just say I failed to get a place - thank goodness!

> ### O POINT OF INTEREST
>
> Grocers Company School was founded in the late nineteenth century by a group of successful East End merchants. It became a highly respected grammar school and probably its most famous old boy is Harold Pinter. In 1966 it became a comprehensive school and after years of controversy it was placed in special measures, and in1995 it closed after more than one hundred years. A victim of sixties ideology.

Woodberry Down Comprehensive School

Even though part of the purpose of grammar schools was to help the children of less wealthy parents gain an education on a par to a public school, because of the requirement to pass the eleven plus, they came to be seen as elitist. The response to this was mixed comprehensive schools where there were no barriers to entry and all levels of ability were admitted. The increase in the number of pupils allowed for more facilities so along with academic ability, vocational ability could be catered for. Woodberry Down Comprehensive School was one of the first of such schools and it opened its doors for the very first time in 1955.

This being a flag ship school, it was built to impress. From its tall class clad entrance foyer to its well-equipped biology, chemistry and physics labs. Along with its vocational workshops kitted out with lathes, milling machines and forges, there was a carpentry workshop. There was an art block. There were kitchens for home economics. There was a commercial department, with row upon row of typewriters. In the grounds there were two purpose built gymnasiums, one for girls and one for boys.

The First Day

Having not being admitted to Grocers grammar school, I was very pleased to be offered a place at Woodberry Down. On the first day I found myself, along with two friends from junior school, in the impressive assembly hall waiting to hear our fate. Two of us were allocated to the same class while the third of was allocated to a different class. We all looked at each other and asked in disbelief,

"Why are they splitting us up?"

The answer was soon revealed when the two of us, sat in our classroom and the form teacher introduced himself,

"My name is Mr Marshawn and although you'll go to different teachers for different lessons, I'm going to be your form teacher for the next three years. This is class 1M and the class initial is taken from my name so that does not disclose the stream you're in. That is not supposed to be known, but I can tell you that you are in the second from top stream and there are nine streams in your year".

So now it became clear; the first stream was for those who had passed the eleven plus easily, the second stream was for those who had narrowly passed, the third stream was for those who had narrowly failed, so on and so forth, until you reached stream nine. Stream nine was for those with learning difficulties.

As for the reason Mr Marshawn chose to break this confidence, I will never know. So our friend, from junior school, remained in the fourth stream, as he had not done as well as his classmates. I remember feeling let down, by what I felt to be a betrayal of fairness, despite the declarations of the comprehensive schools, we were still being graded in academic terms.

The School Structure

There were around thirty pupils in each class, meaning there were two hundred and seventy in year one and the total of pupils in the whole school was around thirteen hundred. The school was divided in four houses named after famous people: Curie house (Marie Curie), Einstein house (Albert Einstein), Keller house (Helen Keller) Scott house (Robert Scott) the idea being to create friendly rivalry (in sport, etc) between the different houses. The motto of the school was 'Fellowship is Life' reflecting the togetherness felt by society at the time.

Carpentry Workshop

> ## ○ POINT OF VIEW
> My belief is that the comprehensive system is neither good nor bad, the catchment area should decide the type of school that is the most appropriate. Because of its number of pupils, Woodberry Down was equipped with fantastic facilities, which attracted good teachers, and it was this that helped make it a very good school. However, the pupils were still streamed according to their academic ability and taught separately most of the time. I did not see the point of it being a comprehensive apart from size and therefore, its facilities.

Childhood Friends

For no reasons I've ever understood, my friends contained themselves in different groups depending on how we came to know each other. So I had friends at school, friends in church and friends where I lived. On the rare occasions when they come across each other there was an invisible wall between us and so we always remained in their separate groups.

School Friends

We only mixed together in school related activities. These included staying behind in the school library to help each other with our homework (cheating) then walking home together and parting when we needed to go our separate ways.

Friends from Church

Apart from Sunday school, there was the Boys Brigade which involved playing in the band, marching, camping holidays and as we grew older, going for a pint in the Londesborough or the Neville Arms. Our group (65th North London Company) normally went camping in a farmer's field in Epping Forest. There were no facilities or home comforts (this is now known as wild camping) and it involved doing such things such as fetching water from the farmhouse in 'billy cans' and finding wood for cooking on an open fire. As city boys we loved being in the open air and we always respected the country code. A fantastic benefit for me was, being away from the polluted air of London, I could run and play freely just like all my mates could do all of the time.

> ○ **POINT OF INTEREST**
>
> In 1963, I was with the Boy's Brigade camping in the Isle of Wight. There were many of us there and we had to take it turns to do jankers (army slang for chores) and my task was to help peel the hundreds of potatoes required. This took a couple of hours and this needed to be done every day. One of the officers, tired of our complaining, explained the previously ordered mechanical potato was stuck on a train that had been delayed for several days. We later found out, that it was the same train at the centre of the Great Train Robbery. After the trial there was a national outcry over the length of the sentences give to the robbers. What isn't well known is that It wasn't just for robbing the train, it was for forcing us to peel hundreds of potatoes by hand!

Friends At Home

As well as all the usual playing, two of my friends were brothers and they had a father who was always full of ideas for things for us to do. So on many occasions, we three would get on our bikes and visit places such as: the British Museum, the Science Museum, the Tower of London, as well as going further afield to: Epping Forest, Potters Bar and as far as St Albans.

We did all this on our bicycles, so it was suggested that we became 'Knights of the Road'. This test was organised by the News of the World, a newspaper that would later spectacularly fall from grace.

So off we cycled to their head office in Fleet Street to make enquiries. I think they were amused to find us three scruffy 'erberts in their plush offices but they reacted well and told us that we'd need to pass the Cycling Proficiency Test (CPT).

So we found out about the next CPT to be organised in our local area. When we passed, the next thing we knew, was that we had become famous! We were mentioned by the local Mayor during a council meeting, a photographer from the Hackney Gazette came round to take some photographs, (one with us cheekily pointing to a 'Cycling Prohibited' notice which was not printed) and I was also praised by my school's headmistress in assembly. All of this was most embarrassing and caused a fellow pupil to make a snide remark,

"What did you do? You only passed the cycling proficiency test; we've all done that."

But it was more than that, it was because we had researched and organised the Knights of the Road process ourselves. Such is the power of the press and it is a further indication of how much independence we were allowed as kids.

O POINT OF VIEW

At the age of fourteen, I sent this joke to the Topper comic. In the Tower of London, one Beefeater is saying to another,

"What's this I hear about you being a vegetarian?"

My joke was printed, and so I won the prize of a penknife. It seems unusual now, that children were trusted and given so much autonomy.

Back To School

At Woodberry Down School, during the third year (year 9), we were given the choice of either: leaving school and starting work at the end of the fourth year (year 10) or continuing at school until the end of the fifth year (year 11) and completing one of the following two-year courses:

1. Commercial course, intended for secretarial work.
2. Technical course, intended for manufacturing and the vocational trades.
3. Academic course, intended for arts, management and maybe staying on until university.

All three courses were designed to equip you for the world of work with only a small percentage expected to go to university. In my class, all of us had passed the eleven plus, but only one of us was encouraged to go to university. This pupil declined the chance, preferring to do the technical course.

I wanted to do the academic course, being interested in history and geography, but on being told that I couldn't do both, I decided to do the technical course instead. A decision which set me on the road to a very enjoyable career in the electrical industry.

In my year, there were around twenty of us doing the technical course and we were aiming to obtain one or more of the following GCEs: English, maths, physics, technical drawing, and metalwork.

The metalwork workshop contained ample work benches along with hand tools, two pillar drills, two grinding machines, a surface grinder, six lathes, a milling machine and a forge. There was a dedicated storeroom with a full-time storekeeper, who issued tools and materials as required.

Following Tony Blair's infamous "education, education, education" speech in the late nineties, I visited a GCSE Craft, Design and Technology (CDT) workshop in a secondary school, only to find there was just one pillar drill and that wasn't even working! In later years, because of the catastrophic lack of workplace skills, training centres were set up in order to provide the vocational training skills that were no longer a realistic part of the secondary schools curriculum.

Strowger Telephone Stepping Switch

O POINT OF VIEW

The hi-jacking of vocational training by educationalists could not be better illustrated than by the BBC programme 'The Great Egg Race' first shown in the nineteen eighties. In true Blue Peter style, it solved engineering problems using things like elastic bands, plastic egg boxes and bits of string. This programme was a slap in the face for true engineers, who spend many years in training and in gaining experience and it helped to ease the way for the removal of vocational training from the secondary schools curriculum.

Lift Control Gear

PART FIVE

THE CUBAN MISSILE CRISIS

The backdrop to these times, always in the background, was the cold war between the Western powers and the USSR. Starting in junior school, we were told of the possibility of a nuclear war and the 'four-minute warning' of an imminent attack. Looking back, I'm astounded that so few people seemed particularly bothered. I suppose it was the wartime spirit of 'carrying on' and the possibility of 'being knocked down by a bus' that put the nuclear threat into the context of how disaster could strike without warning at any time of life.

The World Holds Its Breath

However, the Cuban Missile Crisis brought all this into focus when President Kennedy threatened to blockade Soviet Union ships bringing nuclear missiles to Cuba, close to America's border. The fact that NATO had nuclear missiles in Turkey, on the Soviet border, seems to have been overlooked. So, after the scariest few days in my life, President Khruschev backed down and Kennedy took the credit for being strong and standing up for freedom. The world breathed again. Many years later it was disclosed that the situation was actually resolved through behind-the-scenes diplomatic negotiations, that included NATO removing their missiles from Turkey.

The Swinging Sixties

Social commentators often say,

> *"If you remember the sixties, you weren't there!"*

Well, *I do* remember the sixties and *I was there*! If *you* don't remember the sixties, it's probably because *you weren't there* and are only repeating a meaningless cliché.

Filling Gossip Columns

Actually, the term 'swinging sixties' was a media invention and involved no more than a handful of the 'beautiful' people. These so-called beautiful people mainly consisted of: wannabe pop-stars, failed artists, pretentious actors, unprincipled photographers, newspaper reporters and the idle rich. Swinging London itself was a handful of streets in and around London's West- End, places like: Carnaby Street, Sloane Square and Cheyne Row. All the 'happenings' went mainly unnoticed by ordinary people and was only of interest to shallow and bored sensation seekers. However, away from the hysteria, real developments in music were taking place.

Poplular Music

The rapidly growing influences of American culture originated well before I was born and by the nineteen-fifties they were well established. My earliest memories are of television advertising, brash but fun quiz shows, westerns and magical cartoons (Disney, Tom & Jerry as examples). American popular music was often played on the BBC Light Programme (now unimaginatively called R2) with Frank Sinatra, Doris Day and Burl Ives standing out most in my memory. Lonnie Donegan, a Scottish musician, inspired by American folk music, in turn inspired many young people to form skiffle groups and some went on to became famous pop groups.

Rock'n'roll

But it was Elvis Presley, with Heartbreak Hotel, who was the real game changer and he presaged the short era of genuine rock and roll. Musicians such as Little Richard, Chuck Berry and Duane Eddy (the twang's the thang) introduced Britain to what was happening in America. Rock and roll introduced Britain to many American musicians and British musicians (although some very popular) didn't have the glamour of the Americans. So when I first heard the Beatles on the radio, with their first single 'Love Me Do' I immediately assumed that that the Beatles were American – they were far too good to be British! However, the initial impact of rock and roll had diminished and before the Beatles, there wasn't a lot happening. During this lull, I'd become interested in Classical music played on records, both at home and, while waiting for the assembly to begin at Woodberry Down.

Pop Music

Of course, the Beatles smashed the hit parade wide open and opened the door for the 'Liverpool Sound' which came to be known as beat music. Many other groups followed and some 'popular' music evolved into 'pop' music and pop became a genre all of its own. Mass hysteria which began with films (and probably before) had moved into popular music, with singers such as Frank Sinatra being the focus of attention of mainly young girls. The Beatles brought mass hysteria to Britain and those who wanted to make their fortunes were quick to jump on the band wagon. Pop music and commercialisation became bosom companions.

British Blues

As the sixties wore on, I'd became more and more interested in the development of pop and had taken to visiting pubs where live bands could be heard. These bands usually played cover versions of the hit parade but the standard was extremely poor, both in terms of musicianship and the quality of their sound. So when a friend suggested that brilliant bands regularly appeared in The Hornsey Wood Tavern, I wasn't particularly interested but he insisted that I gave it a try.

The Local Pub

The Hornsey Wood Tavern was a twenty-minute walk from where I lived, an ordinary pub with a function room that was used as a music venue. I arrived at around seven thirty and paid 7/6d (the price of an Indian meal) to enter. Inside it was small, dark and packed with, I guess, around one hundred young people *literally* standing shoulder to shoulder. There was a small stage, dimly lit, and electric blues playing from the loudspeakers. There were large photographs on the walls advertising Ziegfield's Follies, a musical revue from 1907, which seemed to set the atmosphere that was getting more and more excited. Suddenly five musicians strode onto the stage, picked up their instruments and with no introduction the room was filled with the electrifying sound of soaring guitars. This was the first time I heard the sound of genuine Chicago Blues.

Fleetwood Mac

The band was Fleetwood Mac, but not the Fleetwood Mac that would go on to world-wide fame. it was the original Fleetwood Mac, uncommercial and only interested in the genuine sound of American black musicians of the twenties, thirties and forties. There was Mick Fleetwood on drums, John McVie on bass, Peter Green on lead Guitar, Danny Kirwin on second lead guitar and Jeremy Spence on slide guitar. There was a minimum of chat, Peter Green was very friendly but it was all about the blues legends of America. Following the Beatles, American popular music lost its lead to the British, so it's ironic that British musicians were going to take American music back to its homeland. Soon American and British musicians became as one.

Progressive Music

At the same time that blues music was morphing into rock music, folk musicians were using electric instruments to make their traditional music much more exciting. Soul, Gospel and Country Music (not country and western), along with the psychedelic music from California, joined the party and things were getting ready to explode. In 1948, Columbia Records introduced the long playing record (LP) which could play for up to twenty five minutes per side. The LP, otherwise known as an album, freed musicians from the limited playing time of the single and progressive musicians came up with the idea of a concept album. *Sergeant Pepper's Lonely Hearts Club Band* being the first and most famous of them all.

The Isle Of Wight Festival

The year was 1969, it was a Friday evening and I was in the pub having a drink with some of my friends. John, the same friend who had told me about the Hornsey Wood Tavern, was home from university and he suggested that we go to the Isle of Wight because of a music festival taking place over the weekend. The festival had been underway since Friday morning but Bob Dylan was due on stage the next day. So early on Saturday morning, we went to Victoria coach station and caught a coach to Portsmouth. From there we bought a ferry ticket to Ryde, on the Isle of Wight, and from Ryde, along with many others, we walked the rest of the way to the festival site.

Dress Code

The locals seemed pleased to see us, many had set out stalls in their front gardens selling soft drinks and refreshments. Being short of money we bought nothing, thinking we'd get something from inside the festival. I'd previously been camping on the Isle of Wight with the Boy's Brigade, so I felt absolutely at home and supremely confident. At first. John and I didn't look like the 'weekend hippies' and would-be 'flower people' that surrounded us. He was home from university, in his unpretentious charity-shop clothes, wishing we had 'thumbed-it' to Portsmouth, saving much needed money for food. Me, a trainee technician, sporting a tweed jacket, complete with leather elbow patches and a neon-tester in the top pocket. It takes all sorts, but you wouldn't be seeing us in the Sunday papers.

The Crowd

Anyway, the festival had been underway since the day before so the field was jam packed with barely a space to sit down. There were no designated emergency exit routes and to get anywhere, at all, meant treading on people because of the lack of space. The crowd was incredibly relaxed and seemed to be enjoying the disorganisation, cheerfully treading on you and apologising with a cheery, "Sorry man." You were supposed to respond with, "Hey, that's okay man." I never said it but I was thinking, stop apologising and just stop treading on me! The queues for refreshments along with the lavatories, were literally longer than your arm (sic) and so we decided not to bother, and just wait to see if the situation eased up. Getting used to the situation; I started to take things in. Next to us there was a family group who had come with a stash of food all set for a picnic, it was not very into the prevailing 'community spirit' I felt. Having skipped breakfast (by now, it was well into the early afternoon) I started to enviously eye-up their food. I was starving and if I could have got away with it, I would have liberated a pork pie and triangle of sandwich and perhaps they would offer me something to drink,

> "Thanks man, that's really good of you." My fantasy.
> "What are you doing? Are you stealing our food!?"
> Their reality.

No, it was far too risky and there was no chance of running away. I would have needed to tread on, and apologise to, at least a dozen people before I'd gone twenty yards.

The Let Down

So, we'd just have to starve but anyway we're here for the music and we have Bob Dylan to look forward to. Another let down. Bob didn't come on stage until two in the morning! What had he been doing all evening? When the time came, I saw him walk on the stage and I saw him walk off the stage, I slept all the time he was on the stage. So, I completely missed him. But by now it was early morning, time to beat the crowds and get back to London. Those are my memories of the festival that filled the Sunday papers and created many a myth. Sorry to be a party pooper but the next bit is a lot more interesting.

The Isle of Wight Ferry

We had beaten the rush but it was still very busy, as John and I walked back to the ferry. We didn't talk about the music because we'd hardly noticed it! The strident electric guitar riffs, the insistent throb of the base guitar, the long, self-indulgent thrashing of the drum solos (fashionable for a thankfully short period) had not impressed us at all, because these were merely vague noises coming from a distant stage. No, we talked about being starving hungry and where could we get something to eat. We decided to wait until we got back to Portsmouth, because the ferry would be too busy, we were definitely right about that!

Safety First

The first sign of trouble was seeing the walkers, ahead of us, gathering into a crowd. There was a member of the crew, on the upper deck of the ferry, shouting through a loud hailer.

> *"What's happening?" I asked somebody who'd got there before us.*
> *"The captain's saying that there's too many of us and that we'll sink the ferry if we all get on at once. He wants us all to get away from the ferry and come closer a few at a time."*

The message was drove home dramatically by another crew member appearing with a hose and directing a powerful jet of water towards us. There are those amongst us who would sensationalise this occurrence, in order to make a living, but I'll stick to what was really happening. We didn't know at the time, but far more people had arrived for the festival than expected. The captain was concerned about all our safety and had directed the crew member to play the water in *front* of us and not *at* us in order to drive us back. Not a single person got wet and once we had accordingly moved away, we were allowed onto the boat in an orderly manner. *The most telling thing I can say about the festival, is that this was the only example of things being properly organised that we saw.*

Food, Glorious Food

Once on dry land we found a place that was serving breakfast. These were the days before menus were restricted to hamburgers and pizzas, so we chose a traditional English breakfast. I had egg, bacon, beans, tomatoes, two fried slice and a cup of tea. John had sausage, egg, chips and a bottle of Pepsi cola. That was all our money spent. We had return tickets for the coach back to Victoria coach station and from there we walked back to Stoke Newington.

The Reckoning

I arrived home after lunchtime and was greeted by my parents. My dad was waving a copy of the Sunday paper showing a topless girl dancing ecstatically in front of a large crowd.

"What's all this? What have you been doing?"
"I never saw any of that, there was nothing like that going on." I was dismissive.

My dad immediately dropped his guard and my mum was smiling. They knew, from long experience, that newspaper reporting is not to be trusted. They just needed re-affirming.

"Have you had anything to eat?"
"No thanks, Mum, I just want to go to bed."

So, I went to my own comfortable bed and after a good night's sleep, I was ready for work on Monday morning.

Over the years, I've never met anyone who knows what happened at the ferry and yet there must be many who think they know about the topless girl. In director John Ford's film The *Man Who Shot Liberty Valance*, the newspaper editor says,

"When you have to choose between history and legend - print the legend."

The Woodstock Festival

Speaking of legends, although the Isle of Wight festival was the first outdoor rock festival held in September 1968, it was the Woodstock festival in mid-August 1969 that made the headlines. I suppose it's natural to assume that those, living through events, know what is happening around them. Speaking for myself, I had no Idea of the 'big picture' or I might have realised that the amount of publicity given to Woodstock, would lead to the vastly increased crowds at the Isle of Wight festival held a few weeks later. You might say that I couldn't see the 'Wood(stock)' for the trees. I thought I was going to see Bob Dylan, in the same way that that I saw other first-rate acts in my local pubs and clubs. That's how much I knew.

A student Union leader acquaintance, with no background in entertainment, was booking famous acts for 'peanuts' but it wasn't long before 'mega-bucks' became the norm. So my music went from pubs, clubs to massive stadiums and, for me, into oblivion. Hype and commercialism has never been my 'bag' to use a term current at the time.

O POINT OF VIEW

Pop music has become a way of life for many people who are completely immersed in the excitement, the glamour, the gossip, the competitiveness and anything and everything else.

Music festivals are exploited by major industries to sell everything from beef-burgers to fashion clothes and merchandising, once despised as 'hype', is now fully embraced. It's all a very long way from just simply enjoying the music.

Thank goodness there are still many talented musicians playing for love, in pubs, clubs and small venues. Ah, just as it was back in the sixties!

Hornsey Wood Tavern

Playbill 1969

Home of British Blues

Newport Jazz Festival

PART SIX

THE GROWTH OF TECHNOLOGY

As an electrical technician, I was often at the forefront of new developments helping to maintain accommodation plant which is now known as building services. It included: lifts, heating & ventilation, air-conditioning and general electrical installations. The biggest names in those fields includes Express Lifts and Satchwell Controls being British, while Otis Elevators, Carrier and Honeywell are American. The development of micro-electronics was also taking place and I once had the dubious privilege of accidently destroying an early device. It was a *555 timing chip* which at the time costs around £11 (over 300 Mars bars) a far superior and robust version can be bought today, for only a few pence. I echo the hackneyed cliché that they don't make things like they used to. *No, they make them far better!*

Tomorrow's World

Outside of work, technology was also abounding with transistor radios, microwave ovens, ball-point pens, pocket calculators and LED watches. Many of these were spin-offs the space race. A joke at that time, was that the Americans were looking for something that they could use to write in outer space, could write upside down, could withstand extreme variations in temperature and wouldn't leak in zero gravity, so at vast expense they developed the Fisher Space Pen. The Russians, after much research, decided to use a pencil! I was fascinated by the space race and followed it with interest. The television programme Tomorrow's World explained developments in technology in an accessible way and it was a shame when it also fell victim to the domination of academic achievement.

Meanwhile, advances in technology were driving us relentlessly towards the globe village predicted by Marshall McLuhan.

Intercontinental Travel

The Jumbo Jet was the popular name for the Boeing 747 wide bodied aircraft, that first came into service in February 1969. At this time, I'd known Tony for around 12 years, from 1957 when my family moved next-door to his. We were childhood friends and our friendship continued into later life and there's a bit more about Tony later. Although Tony was born in London, both his parents were from Ireland and all his family regularly attended the local Roman Catholic church in Bouverie Road. Although not obviously religious, at a young age, he decided that he wished to become a Catholic Priest and at the age of eighteen he began his training.

Becoming a Catholic Priest

The first year involved attending The Catholic Seminary, in The Netherlands and when he came home for the summer break in July 1969, it was only to tell us that he would soon be off again. As part of the training they were, more or less, told to take a working holiday in America as it would be a very good experience. This holiday was to include spending time in the state of California. According to the seminary authorities, the girls in California found the vows of celibacy, taken by these young men, a definite challenge and it was thought better to test their resilience to temptation before they were too far into their training. Times have changed a lot since those years and I'm writing from memory, so please don't be offended, I may well have misunderstood the situation.

A Walk in the Park

Anyway, holidaying abroad was new to most people and the idea of flying to America in a Jumbo Jet was most exciting. So, along with his fellow seminarians, they flew to New York, to spend a few days, before continuing their journey. Tony had arranged to visit one of his uncles who was a policeman in the New York Police Department (NYPD). That's right Tony's Uncle was a *New York Irish Cop*, the kind of figure we'd only ever seen on television! They'd never met before, so after becoming acquainted with each other, they decided to take a walk in Central Park. His Uncle was dressed in civilian clothes but on their way out he, reached into a drawer, took out a gun and put it into his pocket,

> "That's in case I'm recognised." He said to his nephew, in a matter of fact way.

Tony was shocked by this routine carrying a gun and he was to find out later how accepted this routine was.

Selling Ice Cream

After their time in New York, they were off to Chicago. It was a working holiday so they all needed to find a job and Tony, along with one of his fellow travellers, found a job selling ice-cream from a large, brightly painted van. They were told it wasn't safe to cross over the railway tracks, so of course they did. If it wasn't for the mugger, that was trying to knife him, getting in the way of the mugger that was trying to shoot him, he never would have survived to tell the tale.

The Highway Patrol

They were on the freeway, on their way to California, when they heard the dismal wailing of a police-car siren. Their driver had inadvertently broken the speed limit and they were being pulled over for speeding. If they were expecting the traditional British police response of 'can I see your driving licence sir' they were in for a very rude awakening. This is the USA,

> "Get out of the car!" The uniformed policeman barked as he pointed his gun, "get your hands up and spread your bodies over the hood!"

There were four of them, all young men, and the speed cop was on his own so you can understand his urgent need to control the situation. He rapidly frisked them but on finding them unarmed, his manner became much more relaxed,

"Where y'all headed, in such a rush?"

It was Tony who answered him,

"We're going to San Diego, to the college there,   we're all training to be priests."

"Training to be priests! Why, I thought you were a bunch of hoodlums by the way you were driving." He grinned broadly.

So with the tension eased, everyone saw the funny side of it and after a few laughs, they all continued on their way, their experience of the Highway Patrol having ended better than it started.

Tony's Reflections

Tony told me about these stories on his return. Having been away for over four weeks he was a changed man, more thoughtful and less flippant. I could tell that his experiences had really affected him which, after all, was the purpose of his holiday. So how did he get along with the girls in California? He never spoke about that but he did go on to be ordained and, later, become the parish priest at his local church in Bouverie Road. We'll let the record speak for itself.

My Reflections

I wish to say that all this happened a long time ago and written from my memory. I'm sure that things are very different now. Oh, one last thing, I asked Tony about his experience of flying in a Jumbo jet. Was it the roominess, was it the number of passengers, was it the food, was it the comfort, was it the crew? This is what he told me; the most impressive things are the engines they're big enough for a person to stand up in! So there you have it, big planes have big engines. Who would have guessed it?

> **◯ POINT OF INTEREST**
>
> The Liberty Bell in Philadelphia was made in the Whitechapel Bell Foundry, Mile End, London in 1752. In 1753 it was found to be cracked and so was recast, using the same metal, by American engineers John Pass and John Stow.
>
> The American War of Independence ended in 1776; they won!

International Tourism

The Jumbo Jet made mass tourism possible and the increase in holiday makers was quickly to be seen. Growing up in Inner London, my friends and I often the visited London's famous buildings during the school summer holidays. Of course, these places were busy but nothing like what was to come. After leaving school, my places of work were telephone exchanges along with large office building in and around central London, so I had plenty of opportunities to witness the growth in tourism. What really drove things home for me, was the exhibition of Tutankhamen at the British Museum in 1972, where you needed to queue for up to seven hours. Everywhere you went there were queues and tourist were everywhere. My childhood haunts such as the Tower of London, were packed with people gawping and taking photographs, stopping in large groups to listen to what the tour guide was saying. The underground trains, where you packed like sardines in the rush hours, were sardines throughout the day. Americans were the first and, before long, the whole world followed. Them visiting us and us visiting them. The Jumbo Jet directly affected all our lives, marking the beginnings of global swarming(sic) and turning my town into a holiday destination foreign travel.

Off on holiday!

> ### ○ POINT OF INTEREST
>
> One day I had an embarrassing incident. I was looking for Trafalgar Square and, not knowing the area, I stopped to ask a stranger the way.
>
> "Why it's just at the end of the street, Mac!"
>
> Hearing my London accent, he looked at me with suspicion. Hearing *his* accent, I realised I'd inadvertently asked an American tourist the way. In my hometown, of all places!

Goodbye Bangers and Mash

As could be expected all this tourism led to a change in eating habits. As mentioned earlier, there were plenty of places to eat delicious plain English food but change was on its way. We already had plenty of Chinese restaurants and now there was a growing number of Indian restaurants catering for dining in the evening (usually after the pubs closed!) but in the City of London, there was gap in the market for eating at lunchtime. This gap was met by the Italians with their sandwich bars. Along with the traditional cheese or ham sandwich, now you were overwhelmed by the choice of every conceivable filling. These fillings included new concepts such as sardines and gherkins, tuna and mayonnaise, examples of fillings which are totally normal today. I had my first proper Italian pizza in a restaurant in the West-end, Kentucky Fried Chicken near Finsbury Park, a Macdonald's burger in City Road and a donor kebab in Shoreditch High Street.

In short, this food was appearing everywhere some run by independent entrepreneurs and some by international chains. Sadly, these changes meant a decline in traditional pie and mash with liqueur, jellied eels, pease pudding and saveloys, only good old-fashioned fish and chips has retained its popularity.

> **O POINT OF INTEREST**
>
> Here's a secret for you; if you're ever in Central London there are still a handful of pie and mash shops where you can get a cheap and delicious meal. Keep it under your hat or soon we won't get a seat, it'll be swarming with tourists!

My First Indian Meal

Tony (the one who became a priest) was one of the friends I grew up with and he worked as a shipping agent for a bonded warehouse in St Katherine's Dock by the river Thames. As we regularly enjoyed a pint together, he invited me to meet him, along with one of his work mates, in a pub after work. So, one evening I joined them in the Brown Bear, Leman Street. Leman Street was still in the shadow of its dark Victorian reputation and the Brown Bear was a gloomy, and a little bit sinister, pub. I enjoyed the company of his workmate (Colin) and we all got along well together so after a few pints it seemed a good idea to visit an Indian restaurant where he regularly enjoyed eating Indian food. It is short walk to Brick Lane and so very soon Colin was ushering us through the door of very dodgy looking restaurant. I was later to describe it as an

Indian 'caff' rather than an Indian restaurant as it was exactly like a working man's caff inside. A waiter greeted us,

> "Good evening, sir, it's nice to see you again."
> "Hello, I've brought some friends – they've never had a curry before."
> "That's very nice, let me show you to a table."

I was only used to working men's caffs, so the kitchen tables covered in blue chequered oilcloths together with fluorescent strip lighting, didn't seem any different. The waiter who had greeted us, went through a door at the back leaving one of his colleagues, who looked like a Cliff Richard tribute act, to show us to our seats. It was very quiet as, we were the only ones there, but the silence was broken by the sound of Indian music heralding the return of the head waiter.

> "Are you ready to eat sir?" He spoke to Colin.

We had settled into our seats and the waiter indicated a large whiteboard fixed to one of the walls.

BEEF CURRY AND RICE
MEDIUM OR HOT.
5/6d

Colin spoke to Tony and me,

> "You'd better have the medium, you won't like the hot."
> The menu didn't exactly spoil us for choice so we soon made up our minds.

Colin turned back to the waiter,

> "Two medium curries and one hot for me, oh and three bottles of beer."
> "Would you also like chapatis?"
> "Yes please, three chapatis as well."

The waiter went back through the door to organize our food and before long he returned with three large dinner plates and a tea-towel over his forearm. He wiped the plates with the tea towel and elegantly set them on the table alongside some forks and spoons. The other waiter brought the food, three bowls of curry, three bowls of rice and three chapatis. After indicating to Colin, which was the hot one, they both respectfully retired to let us get on with our meal.

Colin took on the role of mother hen,

"Spread the rice on the plate leaving a well in the centre."

He used his own plate and the rice to demonstrate.

"Now put some of your beef curry into the centre and mix it with the rice, eat with your spoon and fork. Eat the chapati with your fingers."

We fell silent as we began to eat, and the flavours, the music and the aromas combined to make this a completely new experience. Suddenly the heat of the spice hit the back of my throat, and I began to cough. Tony began coughing as well.

"If it's too hot, don't drink the water, that'll make it worse, just mix more rice with the curry or eat your chapati with it." Colin was amused by our reaction but was trying to be helpful.

Tony and I struggled on a bit longer but in the end we both admitted defeat.

"It's absolutely delicious but it's just too hot." Tony spoke to Colin and the waiters who had come to see what was going on.

"It's really nice but I just can't eat any more." I agreed with Tony.

Tony and I were ready to go and we put on our coats, the waiters smiled understandingly and began clearing away the plates.

"See you Colin, it's been a great evening but we have to get back to Stoke Newington. I'll see you in work tomorrow."
"Okay, I'm staying on to finish my curry and finish off the beers. You've hardly touched yours!"

"Goodnight Colin, it was really nice to meet you." I'd had a really good time.

The waiter opened the door and Tony and I stepped out into the darkness of Brick Lane.

> ○ **POINT OF INTEREST**
>
> The price of the meal being five shillings and sixpence (5/6d) is about six pounds today.
>
> In the early days, the price of an Indian meal was roughly the same as an English meal, in a café.

The Walk Home

This was in the days before streetlights were left on all night and before Brick Lane became famous for its Indian restaurants, so this was an adventure for us. My mouth was on fire but by the time we'd walked to the junction of Commercial Street and Shoreditch High Street, the burning sensation suddenly stopped and was replaced by the strangest clean and bright feeling. We turned right and continued walking towards Stoke Newington, it's not very far, and we were home by around midnight. Despite having had many curries since then, I'll never forget my very first curry. I'm happy to say that we had an excellent Indian Restaurant, near where I lived, in Church Street. It was there, guided by the waiters, that I eventually graduated to a *lobster* vindaloo and I never drank the water!

> ○ **POINT OF INTEREST.**
>
> The main road that forms the boundary between Hackney and Stoke Newington, that we called the High Street, is actually the A10 Cambridge Road. Originating at London Bridge, it begins as Gracechurch Street then undergoes several name changes: Bishopsgate, Newton Folgate, Shoreditch High Street, Kingsland Road, Kingsland High Street, Stoke Newington Road, Stoke Newington High Street, Stamford Hill and then onto Tottenham and beyond. So, you can see why we simply called it the High Street!

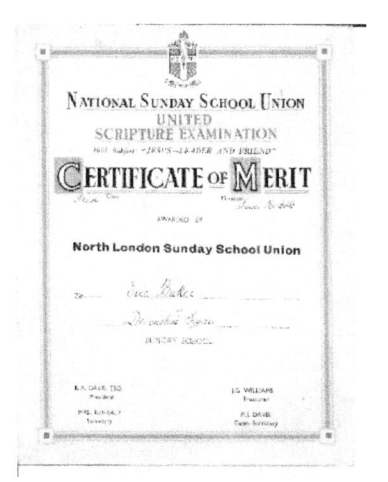

Sunday School Annual Exam.

Boys Brigade Queens Badge.

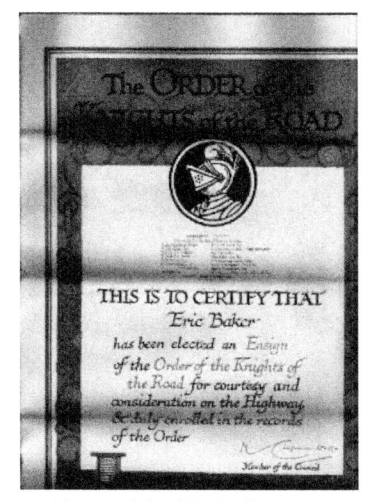

News of the World Scheme.

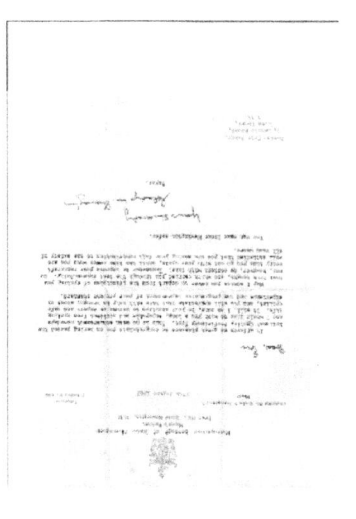

Letter From the Mayor of Stoke Newington.

ERIC BAKER

I'm in the middle, which of my two friends was arrested at gunpoint in the USA?

I'm getting used to school, only four more years to go!

Letter From Ruth Grossman.

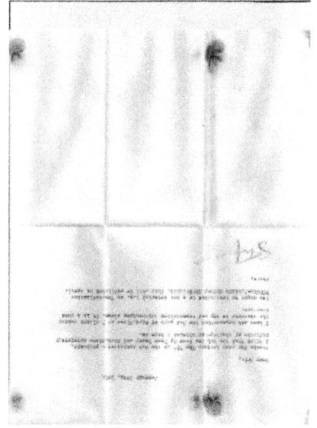

Letter From Stefan Grossman, Legendary Blues Guitar Player.

PART SEVEN

ART

In 1969 I went to an art exhibition at the Heywood Gallery in London called Cybernetic Serendipity. I never did discover what cybernetic serendipity was but I did discover the mysterious world of Renee Magritte and the joyful world of Pop-art. Roy Lichenstein became famous during the sixties along with other American artists such as Andy Warhol.

O POINT OF VIEW

My three selections taken from the most representative works of art of the period:

Chinese Girl, **Vladimir Tretchikoff**, 1952. Also known as the Green Lady, this painting was to be seen on living room walls almost everywhere, along with the flying ducks!

Wham, Roy Lichenstein, 1963. A painting made up from small dots, as if it were the printed page of a comic, complete with speech balloons.

The Son of Man, Rene Magritte, 1964. In the tradition of surrealism, Magritte was notable for his unsettling images.

Cinema

With so many people watching television, the film industry was looking for ways to encourage more people back into the cinemas. One of these developments was Cinerama which used three film screens in order to give a spectacular panoramic view. So, when 'How the West was Won' was showing in London's west-end in 1962 my Dad and I went along to see it. It fully met expectations and we wallowed in the old wild west for an enjoyable time.

We also went to the Circlorama cinema which consisted of eleven screens arranged in a circle and in order to watch the action, the audience stood (not sat) around the centre of the circle with the eleven screens at the circumference. You could look to the left, to the right, to the rear and straight ahead. It literally gave you a pain in the neck and unsurprisingly never caught on.

Size Matters

If I remember correctly, Cinemascope and Panavision became the popular formats and cinema started to attract a young audience. Among my favourites, of those set in America, are Psycho, The Graduate, True Grit along with the Spaghetti Westerns.

Of those set in Britain, A Shot in the Dark, Zulu, and The Italian Job. Before these, I really enjoyed the Ealing Studio style films starring actors such as: Alec Guiness, Peter Sellers, Lionel Jeffries and many other comedy actors.

○ POINT OF VIEW

My three selections taken from the most representative films the period:

I'm Alright Jack, directed by John and Roy Boulting, 1959. A satirical take on how self-interest was replacing the shared purposes of the war years. Set in a large manufacturing business, class warfare was raising its ugly head again. This film is most memorable for Peter Sellers' portrayal of an officious yet idealistic, trade union official.

Blow Up, directed by **Michelangelo Antonioni**, 1966. Made at the high point of flower-power and fashionable hedonism, this film reveals the callousness and shallowness at the heart of the swinging sixties.

Midnight Cowboy, directed by John Schlesinger, 1969. When a naïve but handsome country-boy makes his way to New York to make a good living as a stud, he doesn't know what he's letting himself in for. Used and abused by the jaded rich, looking for fresh meat, he is no match for their cynicism. Luckily, he has made a friend in the destitute but street-wise 'Ratso' and together they make their way to Miami, but it's too late to save them from their destiny. A very intelligent film, with a very poignant end.

Books

I also very much enjoyed reading. As mentioned earlier, I started with Rupert the Bear, moved on through the comics, first British; the Dandy, The Beano, the Topper, then American: with Superman and Batman. My interest in reading books started with Sherlock Holmes and moved on to the modern classics. Billy Liar, Catch 22, Steppenwolf, The Trial, The Ginger Man and 1984 just to name a few of them.

> ### O POINT OF VIEW
> My three selections taken from the most representative books of the period:
>
> The Autobiography of a Supertramp, W H Davies, 1908. The poet W H Davies was born in Wales but spent much time travelling as a tramp in the depression years of the USA. The is an extra-ordinary book which became a firm favourite of thinking youngsters in the 1960s.
>
> Lucky Jim, Kingsley Amis, 1954. By far and away the funniest book I have ever read, Set in a red-brick university in the early 1950s, apart from its hilarity, it sounds an early warning about the lowering of academic standards.
>
> The Third Policeman, Flann O'Brien, 1966. Mixing a real understanding of physics with the ridiculous conclusions of misunderstanding physics, this novel takes you to a fantastic world of madness. It took me many readings to realise what was actually happening.

The Growth of Television

I have never known a time without television and my earliest memories are that, at first, it was very different from today. It was only on for a few hours a day, and was a much calmer, considered experience playing second fiddle to BBC radio.

Reality Television

In the fifties and sixties there was a move to 'kitchen sink' drama and the rise of 'angry young men' playwrights and authors who strove to achieve realism in their work. While there were many landmark plays and books, which were vibrant in their day, over the years 'reality TV' has taken hold because it fills the time, is cheap to make and are job creation schemes for the many wannabees. Adopted from the USA banality began with the soap operas, with their cultural appropriation of so-called working class values together with the overkill of cookery programmes, quiz shows and game shows.

Ticking Boxes

There are many excellent programmes, mainly shown away from prime viewing times, these are for the more discerning viewers and to comply with the regulators. For these, I use my television recorder combined with its remote control, to skip the unwanted stuff. I find myself watching less and less television and I am gradually joining the growing numbers who don't watch television at all. With the growth of technology television is competing with an enormous amount of competition and although much of it is good, it is losing relevance particularly for the young.

> ### ○ POINT OF INTEREST
>
> For anyone who knows London, Albert Square in television's Eastenders, is clearly not set in London's East End. The architecture is typical of the better-off working-class areas and for me, who grew up in **Walford Road**, the name of the fictional borough of **Walford** is the clue. A little research shows that Albert Square is modelled on Fassett Square in Dalston, which is close to Walford Road but over a mile from the East End. A mile in London is a very long way; it can take you from the deprivation to the rear of Euston Railway Station to the wealth of Hampstead Village.

Advertising

The first indication that big business had seen the power of television, from what was happening in America, was when Associated Rediffusion began to show programmes for Independent Television (ITV) in 1955. This permitted the use of adverts and allowed for the less 'stuffy' programmes than were perceived to be made by the BBC.

I probably have been subconsciously influenced by television commercials because it is so pervasive, but I have rarely bought anything as a direct result of watching a commercial. Over my lifetime I have spent less than £200, I once bought a chocolate bar and on another occasion £150 on a vacuum cleaner, but that's it.

Television News

During the war, radio news readers were an essential part of the war effort and with the arrival of television they became household names. Their prestige was passed on to the next generation and gradually they have taken their lead from the United States and news readers became national heroes. Reporting from outside news locations, for no other reason that that's how it's done in America, regardless of the waste of resources and the inconveniences. To paraphrase Parkingson's Law; News spreads to fill the available time. News items are decided by shadowy figures who never explain the reasons for their decisions. News 'values' are very controversial regarding relevance and taste.

The Fight

It was around 1964 when a young lad I knew was on his way to a gang fight that was to happen a few streets away. He showed me the machete he was carrying and cheerily asked if I wanted to come along, needless to say I declined. He returned around thirty minutes later covered in blood, explaining the person he had taken a swing at, had turned the machete back on him. He showed me the large gash across his face, he sported with pride, while ignoring the pain he must have been feeling. He told me, the police had arrived, broken up the fight and then everyone scarpered for fear of arrest.

It's Not News

The fight went unreported by the national press, television and even the local newspaper gave it a miss. Gang fights happened from time to time but, because they usually went unreported, there was no copycat effect. It was all over as quickly as it started. To paraphrase Parkingson's Law, news spreads to fill the available time. News items are decided by shadowy figures who never explain the reasons for their decisions and news 'values' are very controversial regarding relevance and taste. Some things are best left unsaid and freedom of the press, includes reporting responsibly.

O POINT OF INTEREST

News is not a solid item such as a brick. The word *news* is an abstract noun and can mean anything you want it to mean.

What's shown in news programmes is not all of what actually happened (that's impossible - too much has happened) it's a selection taken from all the things that have happened.

So, items of news are choices made by an editor; they are not solid items like bricks.

British Pathe News

British Television

I only ever watched a few things on television but what I watched, I enjoyed.

> ### ○ POINT OF VIEW
>
> My three selections taken from the most representative television shows of the period:
>
> Coronation Street 1960 and still running. Although I never watched a single episode, I was fully aware of the names Ena Sharples and Hilda Ogden, such was its popularity. In 1997 I watched an episode to see what all the fuss was about, I could see why it has a following, but it was not my cup of tea.
>
> Steptoe and Son first shown 1962. A father (Albert) and his middle-aged son (Harold) are rag and bone men with a horse and cart. As a dying breed they struggle to make a living but while Albert is content to scrape along, Harold has his sights set on higher things. The generation gap is the cause of much hilarity and sadness.
>
> Monty Python's Flying Circus 1969 – 1974. In the tradition of the Marx Brothers, The Goon Show and the Cambridge Footlights, many of the sketches were side splittingly funny. What's forgotten now, is that equally as many sketches were extremely tedious, when you've seen one foot stamping on the head of a statue, you've seen the lot.

American TV Shows

Many American television shows are hugely entertaining and my favourites are the 'cops' genre and includes Highway Patrol, Dragnet, Colombo and Monk. Also comedy shows such as, I Love Lucy, Mary Tyler Moore and Rowan & Martin's Laugh-in. There was also a very strong influence on quiz shows with their emphasis on pizzazz and lots of cash. Although I preferred the one-time sedate BBC, I appreciated the livelier input from American television along with 'Americanised' commercial television.

The Satire Boom

My first memory of satire on television was 'That Was the Week That Was' (TW3). I was too young to really take it in but I gathered that adults thought it brilliant and groundbreaking, mainly because it featured an impression of the then Prime Minister Harold Macmillan. On my seeing old broadcasts as an adult, it comes across as being predictable, self-satisfied and childish. My preference was the American show Rowan and Martin's Laugh In, which featured the still popular Goldie Hawn. Part of the satire boom was Private Eye, a satirical magazine that I still subscribe to.

Comedy

At this time stand-up comedians became popular, possibly inspired by the *Dave Allen At Large* show. What I find most notable is that their 'biting observations' are reserved for safe targets such as politicians or the royal family, never on each other or potential employers.

> **O POINT OF VIEW**
>
> There is lots of funny stuff but most comedians cease to be funny once they start getting on a bit. Once you give a dog a good name it can live on its merits for ever and audiences will laugh at anything when they've decided that you are funny.

Town Planning

During the post-war years, there was a lot of re-development going on all around me. This need was brought about because of the bombing, the development of the motor car and the expectation of a higher living standard. Unfortunately, the architects and town planners of the time, had little knowledge of London (and other cities) or of working-class lives.

They were often driven by financial considerations or the admiration of their peers. Fortunately Stoke Newington (still like a village even to this day) escaped the worst excesses of high-rise flats and inner-city road development. The bombing of the docks in East London was held by some to be a good thing, as it cleared the slums, but many thought that town planners were causing more damage to London than the Luftwaffe ever dreamed of.

> O **POINT OF VIEW**
> Since those times thanks to people such as, the then Prince of Wales (monstrous carbuncle!!) and Sir John Betjeman with his love of domestic architecture, modern developments are more in keeping with what is needed.

Capital Punishment

Following some controversial hangings, capital punishment was suspended in 1964 and in 1969 was made permanent. This was a very contentious issue between those who thought it was a deterrent and those who thought the risk of hanging an innocent person (being irreversible) is too great.

> O **POINT OF VIEW**
> The thing I noticed, was that when an accused person was found guilty of murder and then executed, there was a feeling of closure and that the price had been paid for the crime. Whereas following abolishment and solely a prison term was to be served, there was a feeling of dissatisfaction and resentment. Added to which, I noticed there was a feeling of personal *dislike* for the felons, a feeling of dislike I'd not noticed before.

Censorship

Keith Waterhouse's book, *Billy Liar* was first published in 1959. It is a very funny and insightful novel that is intelligently written with many layers of meaning. In the book, Billy Liar's father frequently uses the word 'bloody' (a mild swear word at the time) which the author used to show the father's ignorance and lack of imagination. However, the word bloody was picked-up on by the chattering classes. This kind of storm in a teacup, along with ridicule by leading commentators, helped to bring in a relaxation of censorship in the world of art.

The Outcomes

This relaxation was supposed to herald the dawning of the age of Aquarius and the stage musical 'Hair' was the mundane expression of this new age. The real changes were in the number of nude actors on stage and screen along with rise in explicitness of the 'top-shelf' magazines.

London's west-end became home to criminality along with commercialised sex to the point of when walking home with my dad in the daytime, after watching 'How the West was Won' he was invited into a strip-club despite clearly being with his eleven year old son!

"Care to come inside sir?"

○ **POINT OF INTEREST**

Around this time, I was in Southend-on-Sea on holiday with my mum and dad and we decided to go to the local theatre to watch a production of Billy Liar. Although I enjoyed reading the book when I was older, at that time, I was too young to really enjoy it. The notable thing was that on the way out the theatre manager, seeing my parents were with young children, asked if they had been offended by the language (just the word bloody, remember). They seemed surprised to be asked and seemed to find the question amusing, so they responded that they didn't mind. Like any intelligent people they realised this play was fun and a well observed account of Billy Liar's situation, it was not a license for the excesses that were to come.

The Dawning of the Age of Aquarius?

PART EIGHT

LOOKING OVER MY SHOULDER

> **O POINT OF INTEREST**
>
> In 1946, BBC Television resumed broadcasting in post-war Britain.
>
> In 1962, the first ever live transmission of TV signals between two continents, via an artificial satellite, took place. In the same year, the Canadian philosopher Marshall McLuhan, stated that the world is a global village, based on advances in technology and communications.
>
> In 1969, the first moon landing took place. This massive achievement was the outcome of the joint efforts of many nations and was seen on television by viewers around the world.
>
> In 1971, the influential American artist Andy Warhol predicted, "In the future, everyone in the world will get a chance to be famous for fifteen minutes."
>
> In 1991, what we would recognize as the internet today, became available for public access.
>
> In 1849, the French critic Alphonse Karr wrote, "The more things change, the more they stay the same."

Having come to the end of my reminiscences, I think it's time for looking back at the major changes that have taken place in the forty-five years of the post-war period. In the light of all these fantastic developments I've often wondered just how many things have changed and what have been the changes.

There's undoubtedly been a lot of change but not all change is progress. While there have been enormous benefits, there are also costs to consider. It often feels like two steps forward, one step back. For me the two most demanding issues are, the overwhelming amount of technology and the sheer onslaught of information. My experiences have helped me to develop the survival strategies of scepticism and finding things out for myself.

Scepticism

I love the homely wisdom of the past and *'believe half of what you see and nothing of what you hear'* is one of my favourite sayings. I use scepticism carefully, it's a very powerful way of thinking that is not aways appropriate. I reserve it for politicians, reporters, stand-up comedians and others desperate for our attention. For family and friends, I trust them, and take what they say at face value. Here's how I think about those telling me (selling me?) something:

- Who is giving me this information?
- Why are they giving me this information?
- Who do they represent?
- Who is paying their wages?
- Who has given them their status?
- Why should I believe them?

Clichés

At school, I thought bullying was the occasional times when boys got beat-up and girls had their hair pulled out. I've since learned that bullying is very widespread and it's insidious. It's not just a smack in the gob!   I define bullying as being told what to do and/or told what to think. The use of clichés is often the tool used to influence others. Clichés are very dangerous because, when they are repeated often enough, many people believe they are facts. I've made a list clichés that are used without thought.

> ### ○ POINT OF VIEW
>
> The worst offenders:
>
> "I'm entitled to my opinion." You are entitled to your opinion if you keep it to yourself. If you voice your opinion it must be supported by facts and hard evidence. *You are not entitled to your opinion, in my opinion.* Deadlock!
>
> "I am only being honest." Claimed by someone being offensive. They're not being honest they are slyly stating their opinion. *To which they are not entitled.*
>
> "I have the right to freedom of speech." Freedom of speech is a political freedom not a social freedom. It does not entitle anyone to be abusive, spread lies or cause offence.

Ignorance is Bliss

The term 'ignorance is bliss' is usually taken to mean burying ones head in the sand. However 'ignorance is bliss' is not the full saying.

> **O POINT OF INTEREST**
>
> Thomas Gray said in 1742: "*Where ignorance is bliss,* 'tis folly to be wise."
>
> This means that if you don't *need* to be told something, then you are better off not knowing it.

So, I don't slavishly tune into the onslaught of news information, most of which will never directly affect me. Unsettling myself will not help anyone and so I address myself to the things that do directly concern me.

Cynicism

Cynicism is often confused with scepticism but they are not the same thing. If anything, they are opposites. There are many bullies who deliberately encourage cynicism in order to create a lack of trust in politicians. A lack of trust in one politician, can be exploited by another politician. Cynicism is a form of mental depression, so I try never to be cynical.

> **O POINT OF INTEREST**
>
> The playwright, Oscar Wilde stated that a cynic knows the price of everything and the value of nothing. Cynics *always* predict the worst even though the vast majority of things turn out well. Cynics claim they are only being realistic. Given that most things turn out well, optimists are the ones being realistic.

Doing My Thing

I steer clear of prime time television and I don't read mainstream newspapers. Apart from close family, I don't follow social media. I do what interests me and find out, for myself, the things I want to know. The fantastic thing about modern technology is that the world is literally at our fingertips and the jet engine has made us neighbours across the world. So I certainly do not bury my head in the sand. I think for myself and I don't fill my head with an amount of rubbish, it would take a forklift truck to shift.

Socrates. The ancient Greek philosopher famous for his questioning of everything.

USSR

NATO

EUROPEAN UNION

EARTH

AFTERWORD

I stated in the foreword; this is a post-war history written by a partial, prejudiced and ignorant historian. I have tried to convey how global events changed my small world in a bit-by-bit way and I admit to prejudices, along with errors, unknowingly made.

I surprised myself, in realising just how many memories I have tucked away. I am secure in the knowledge, that some things I remember are not in line with what's generally thought. That's tough, I stand by my recollections!

I hope you enjoyed my journey riding alongside me, perhaps you've surprised yourself by how much you remember along with me too.

If this has been 'before your time' I hope you enjoyed finding out about the things that helped to shape you, along with the world you live in today.

Also, these are my selections taken from the post-war years; they are not bricks! I've enjoyed going over old times and refreshing my memory and I hope that you've too, have enjoyed the ride alongside me.

The Blue Dot.

This photograph of Earth, taken by Voyager 1, is from beyond Neptune and 3.67 billion miles from the sun. 1990.

The astronomer Carl Sagan said, "Look again at this dot. That's here. That's home. That's us."

I'll leave the last words to Bugs Bunny,

That's all folks!